'A welcome resource for practitioners that combines theory, practice and implementation or the why, how and what of how to develop autonomous learners. This book will help you identify your starting point, navigate implementation at a time of hyper change and know that you've had an impact.'

Sarah Philp, Psychologist, Coach and Educator

HOW TO CREATE AUTONOMOUS LEARNERS

To achieve their full potential, it is essential that children develop skills to become autonomous learners, yet this skill does not come naturally to many learners. This book is a practical teaching and planning guide to the theory, practice, and implementation of evidence-based approaches to develop essential metacognitive and self-study skills.

How to Create Autonomous Learners explains how to get students, parents, and partners on board and how to implement these ideas across a class, school, or consortium. Areas covered include:

- How to get children and young people ready to learn.
- Why it is important to teach learning strategies.
- Encouraging children to become more active in the process of learning while also nurturing the development of creativity.
- How to harness learner motivation as metacognition and motivation are highly linked.

Easily applicable in any classroom, this essential resource supports children's development of important metacognitive, self-regulatory, and self-study skills and provides teachers and school leaders with evidence-based approaches for implementing these ideas with the support of parents, students, and partners.

Taryn Moir is a Practitioner Senior Educational Psychologist practicing within a local authority and responsible for project work, policy development, and in-service training for a large number of primary and secondary schools. She was a lecturer on the Educational Psychology course at the University of Strathclyde and is now an assessor and supervisor for the Level 2 Qualification of Educational Psychology Scotland. Taryn is also Review Editor for two international journals: *Frontiers in Education*, Special Educational Needs section, and *Cogent Education*.

HOW TO CREATE AUTONOMOUS LEARNERS

Teaching metacognitive,
self-regulatory and study skills
– a practitioner's guide

Taryn Moir

Routledge
Taylor & Francis Group

LONDON AND NEW YORK

Cover image: © Getty Images

First published 2023
by Routledge
4 Park Square, Milton Park, Abingdon, Oxon OX14 4RN

and by Routledge
605 Third Avenue, New York, NY 10158

Routledge is an imprint of the Taylor & Francis Group, an informa business

British Library Cataloguing-in-Publication Data
A catalogue record for this book is available from the British Library

ISBN: 978-1-032-32582-8 (hbk)
ISBN: 978-1-032-32583-5 (pbk)
ISBN: 978-1-003-31572-8 (ebk)

DOI: 10.4324/9781003315728

Typeset in Interstate
by Apex CoVantage, LLC

Printed in the United Kingdom
by Henry Ling Limited

Dedicated to Drew. Without you I'd be lost.

CONTENTS

ACKNOWLEDGEMENTS

There are a few people who without their support, this work would not have been achievable. I would start by thanking Nicola Stewart and all the other truly inspirational Educational Psychologists within East Ayrshire. They alongside other East Ayrshire staff including Julie Muir, Gail Elder, Heather Vass, and Carol Colville offered invaluable support and encouragement at the conception stages of this study. Thank you.

A huge thank you to Sam March who believed in the added value of this project within the North Ayrshire context. He championed its development within the authority and encouraged me through difficult times. Thanks also to all the extraordinary Educational Psychologists within North Ayrshire who could not have been more supportive. A special mention goes to Sue, Xanthe, Morag, and Craig.

A special thank you to Ceri Stewart, who assisted with the pre- and post-test assessment process and generally provided irreplaceable input. Thanks also to Iain Walker, Fiona Elliot-Frew and Claire MacKenzie, who, with the agreement of Andrew McClelland and Luoana Santarossa were also instrumental to the assessment process described in Chapter 4.

Thanks to the Scottish Division of Educational Psychologists of the British Psychological Society who supported me to share some of this learning more widely at the International School Psychologists Association conference.

Thanks also goes to Ruth Binks, Michael Roach, Laurence Reilly, Jayne Johnson, Lisa McFadden, Karen McPherson, Daniela Cubeddu, Scott Chalmers, John Niven, Michelle Keith, Erin McQuillen, Mark Coyle, Liz Sommerville, Kate Watson and everyone else in Inverclyde Education Service for ensuring that Inverclyde is a wonderful place to work, flourish and continually grow professionally.

A special thank you to Professor James Boyle of Strathclyde University, who provided a level of challenge and support that I have learned greatly from. Also, thanks to Professor Lisa Marks Woolfson and Dr Marc Obonsawin who were there for me before and after my studies. Thanks also go to Professor Elspeth McCartney and Professor Sue Ellis who along with Professor James Boyle undertook the original Scottish feasibility study in 2015 and allowed me to follow up on their research. Thanks also goes to Dr Barbara Kelly taught me so much about implementation science.

Thank you to Dr Alan Haughey, Lesley Arthur, and Ian Wallace who provided advice and assistance in turning my original study and additional learning into a book. Also to Sarah Philp who has always been there to turn to when I needed advice.

Thank you to all my friends and family who had faith in my abilities. Especially, Jasmine, Joyce, Teddy, Carmen, Harrison, and Theo. Also thanks to my tango family who help keep me sane. Last but by no means least to my husband, Drew. You have always believed in me and in all honestly, there is no way I could have achieved anything without you. Thank you, I love you.

1 Introduction and orientation

In 2020, the Covid-19 crisis forced educators to reassess how we teach and educate our children and young people. For until this point, a classroom of 2019 could look very similar to one of 1919. With a teacher sitting at the front of the room with a white rather than black board and children in rows or grouped together facing the front. During the pandemic full-time schooling was not available to all. Parents gained a newfound understanding of the difficulties of teaching their children. Teachers struggled to connect with children and families via online platforms. We all struggled and with various degrees of success, learned to adapt to the strange situation.

While we hope this situation will never happen again, it has reinforced what we already thought – that children need to develop the skills necessary to become autonomous learners. When children reach high school, we often make assumptions that children know how to study, learn, and work independently. Yet, all too often, our expectations as teachers, parents, or educators fall short of the reality. For while it is possible for some children to learn how to develop these skills independently, the use of strategies does not come naturally to many young learners. Increasingly, there is a realisation within education that learning strategies and skills need to be explicitly taught and often our efforts to teach independent learning skills fall short of being effective.

The Covid crisis forced adults, children, and young people to be taught in online platforms. This trend is likely to stay, at least in part. Therefore, this book will show how we, as teachers and educators, can best prepare our children for the brave new world that education systems are gradually moving towards. We know that, for traditional learning settings, self-regulated learning strategies lead to academic achievement. We also now know that when learning online, it is even more important that our children have these self-regulatory, metacognitive, and self-study skills. This book will fully equip the reader to know how to teach metacognitive, cognitive, and study skills during your face-to-face time with learners, so that when they are studying online or at home, they have all the skills and strategies needed to become effective autonomous learners.

We will explore some questions that you may have regarding theory. Questions like, what does the evidence say regarding learning and teaching? What are evidence-based metacognitive, self-regulatory, and self-study skills? What is the research around strategy instruction? What is the difference between a cognitive strategy and a metacognitive strategy?

DOI: 10.4324/9781003315728-1

You may also have questions about the practice. For instance, which metacognitive strategies need to be taught? What other skills need to be taught? How do I teach them? Children are told to use strategies, but that is not enough. We need to teach strategies through a gradual release of responsibility in which the teacher first introduces that strategy, explains how to use the strategy, and then gives students more and more ownership in practicing and applying the strategy over time. We will look at this process in detail.

Finally, you might also have questions about the implementation. How do I roll this out within my school or authority? How do I support parents and pupils? How do I get partners involved? Having information on what makes up effective instruction is not sufficient if we want to roll out an intervention to an entire school or local authority area. We also need to understand how to do this and we will use the lessons learnt in the study of implementation science in order to do so.

Key ideas and themes throughout the book that we will explore

- How do we create the optimum learning environment so children want to learn? We need to ensure that the learning environment feels safe for learning to take place, as the links between motivation and learning are very strong. A learner needs to have the desire to improve their work or comprehension before they are likely to employ any metacognitive repair strategy.
- Why is it important to teach strategies? While all children benefit from effective explicit instruction of a strategy and its use, this process has the potential to reduce the inequalities experienced by disadvantaged learners, raising attainment for all.
- It is not enough to teach subject content. Learners also need to understand the "how" or the process to enable them to successfully complete a task. Also, we need to give our learners a clear understanding of what a successful completed piece of work looks like. Take away the mystery and give them some guidelines and examples.
- When we teach a new strategy, it is not enough to describe it once. Effective instruction in strategies requires a series of steps. Each step moves towards the teacher having less and the learner having more responsibility for implementing their strategy use independently.
- The teacher's explicit teaching and modelling of the use of a strategy illustrates to learners how effective these approaches are and gives them confidence to use them independently. This makes children far more engaged in their own learning process.
- Giving children cognitive and metacognitive strategies is like offering them the learning tools they need for lifelong learning.
- As Shanahan et al. stated in 2010, "Strategies are not the same as the skills typically listed in core programs, nor are they teaching activities. A strategy is an intentional mental action during learning that improves understanding. It is deliberate efforts by learners to better understand or remember what is being learnt".
- Study skills are best taught in the context of real subject-specific tasks rather than as an abstract or discrete topic.
- Students learn best when they are encouraged to create their own notes and reminders. This makes them committed to their learning rather than encouraging

them to be sedentary when a teacher overscaffolds by producing additional materials. Materials the learner creates will be more personalised and therefore more meaningful.

- For these ideas to have an optimal impact, they need to be implemented successfully.
- Successful implementation requires the support of children, parents, and partners.

Book organisation

The book is divided into three parts with:

- Part 1 THEORY. This is concerned with the theory and evidence that supports the assertions and approaches outlined in the book.
- Part 2 PRACTICE. This is concerned with understanding strategies, which ones to teach and how to teach them.
- Part 3 IMPLEMENTATION. This is concerned with implementation and how to successfully embed these approaches at an entire school or authority level.

To get the most out of the book, I hope you will read through it in sequence. However, it can be read by going to the sections which you believe may fit best with your needs. Therefore, in order to help with this process, here are the chapter contents briefly outlined.

Part 1: Theory

Chapter 2: Theoretical models

Why is learning so complex? What do I, as a teacher, need to think about? This chapter aims to make links between theory into practice by introducing some prominent models which have been used to inform practices within the classroom. Reading is one of the first skills that is taught in schools. As we progress, we rely on these reading skills to where learning to read becomes reading to learn. Such a vital skill is ongoing throughout life. The aim of reading is to make sense of (or comprehend) what we read, which often in schools is a variety of different subject's textbooks and handouts. Recognising the importance of reading as an essential study skill, it will be the example used to help make the connections between theory and practice. We will discuss how metacognitive and sociocultural models provide clues that can enhance our understanding of what potentially supports learning within the classroom.

Chapter 3: Research into strategy instruction

This chapter looks at the theory around strategies and discusses the complexity of what makes up a strategy. We will learn about effect sizes to help understand efficacy of different approaches that have been studied in meta-analysis. As studies have recommended that we should take multiple methods to optimise learning, we compare some programmes which take this multiple approach. This favorably highlights the benefits of the approach and pedagogy taken in Chapter 4 and Part 2 of this book.

Chapter 4: UK research

Metacognition, self-regulated learning, and study skills are effective when used across the curriculum. This chapter will look at a piece of research which built upon existing studies mentioned in Chapter 3 and evidenced their effectiveness within the UK context. We will track the school's journeys as teachers attended training and implemented its ideas with the support of a coaching model. The chapter will discuss how the programme was evaluated with outcomes showing it as highly effective across all outcome measures. We will discuss how teachers felt about learning and using this approach. The chapter will discuss implications that other schools may wish to consider when rolling out a similar metacognitive, self-regulatory study skills approach as outlined in Part 2.

Part 2: Practice and pedagogy

Chapter 5: Metacognition and mindset

We will start by considering what metacognition is and discuss why metacognitive skills are important, especially when we want to encourage our children to work independently, either at home or within school. This includes a look at what mindset is, how it develops and how we can support children to develop a growth mindset where we are open to learning new ideas. We will also look at the metacognitive cycle of learning and define what metacognitive strategies are and why it is so important that they be taught explicitly. We also consider some of the subliminal messages that may reinforce or undermine the development of a growth mindset.

Chapter 6: Metacognition and motivation

This chapter considers how metacognition links with motivation and offers some practical ideas about how to get children in the right place to learn. We talk about attunement and the importance of positive and inclusive environments and relationship-based approaches in enabling learners to achieve. We consider how to ensure that the task is set at the right level for optimum learning and through the use of pre-topic self-assessment tasks, we ensure that all children have equal opportunities to access the new learning by ensuring that fundamental vocabulary is understood. When you read this chapter, it might be useful to reflect upon how the models outlined in Chapter 2 are seen in practice.

Chapter 7: How should I teach a strategy?

Within this chapter, we will discuss how to teach a strategy. Effective instruction in strategies includes a series of steps. Although there are several models, we will refer to a seven-step approach in detail. There will be some ideas around the pace of progression and also putting each of the stages into practice. We will discuss how a teacher should periodically review the purpose of any strategy and scaffold children's understanding until they can apply it independently. When a child knows and uses a strategy, we consider the importance of referring to these learnt approaches alongside new ones. It is much more important to learn one or two strategies well than many superficially, and therefore, the process should not be rushed.

Chapter 8: Metacognitive strategies and how to teach them

This chapter will drill deeper into the use of a few particularly useful metacognitive strategies. These are ones which were identified in the research in Chapters 3 and 4. This includes visualising, hearing a voice reading aloud in your head, retelling, summarising, linking, holding your thoughts as you read, questioning, what to do when you don't understand, thinking about the "crunch" points and wondering. Some strategies: "visualise", "link to the wider world", and "questioning" have extensive examples illustrating what teaching them could look like in practice. This will hopefully give you the practitioner ideas about how to implement the other strategies mentioned. We will discuss what these strategies are and how to teach them so that children will feel confident enough to use these strategies independently.

Chapter 9: What cognitive strategies should I teach?

There are lots of cognitive strategies we use. When we are learning a new strategy, there will be the conscious effort involved in employing it. This chapter will discuss how to select the best strategy to teach for your context and how we can do this within a busy curriculum with competing priorities. The pros and cons of structural aids will be discussed and examples will be given. We will discuss how integrating the learning of a new strategy should be done at the same time as teaching content and we will discuss the process and product of learning.

Chapter 10: Successful study skills

Exams form a passageway on to life beyond schools. This chapter explores how we can best prepare our children for all the exams that they will be facing. We will explore how to contextualise study skills so that they are most likely to be employed. This will be by offering concrete subject-specific examples rather than general or abstract advice. This chapter will consider how we can optimise the success of our learners. We will discuss the best ways to study and look in more detail at ways to support children and offer some ideas on how to motivate children.

Part 3: Implementation at the whole school or authority level

Chapter 11: Whole school implementation

This chapter will ask how school leaders can implement these ideas successfully so that we can take an entire school approach to ensuring consistency throughout a child's school years. The ideas in this book are grounded in theory and have been evidenced as being of high impact on raising attainment in schools. We learn that effective implementation is as important as having an evidenced-based approach. The chapter will discuss what good implementation should look like and offer a framework that supports successful implementation of this book's approach at a whole school/authority level, more likely to yield positive results. We will go through each stage of the framework to address the challenges in implementation and how to ensure effective planning and evaluation.

Chapter 12: Pupil participation

The approaches within this book often rely upon quality discussions and when this was evident, the impact on learning was the same as that of the lesser able as it was for those more able. Therefore, the approach can be defined as universal – it increases the attainment of all. Therefore, this chapter begins by considering why we need to have an inclusive environment, what one would look like, and how we can ensure that all children meaningfully take part in group/class discussion. We will discuss effective scaffolding that maximises student potential, how to co-create learning goals, how to support children's understanding of themselves as learners, and some basic information about learning that should be discussed with your learners. This chapter finishes with some ideas on how to lead these general learning discussions.

Chapter 13: Parental engagement

To help support effective implementation of this metacognitive approach to teaching (or indeed any approach), it is essential to bring parents and carers with us. They can offer tremendous support for children at home studying and rarely know how to best help them. This chapter will focus on how to get meaningful parental engagement: how to develop a relationship with parents and how to reach out to parents who are often considered the hardest to reach. We will then consider what key information about the book's approach should be shared with parents/families.

Chapter 14: Professional collaboration and a shout out for educational psychologists

Traditionally, teachers worked very much as individuals. This could be stressful for the teacher, who had nobody to share ideas with. Lack of professional discussion can also make a child's progression through school disjointed. This chapter will start by considering the benefits of professional collaboration before discussing how colleagues and other partners, including educational psychologists, can help support schools in the implementation of the approach within this book.

Chapter 15: Some final thoughts

This chapter will finish by considering how important the skills discussed in this book are, not only for lifelong learning, but for our ability to function well within society.

Learning through self-reflection

Hopefully, you will build upon your current practice by using some ideas in each chapter, making your role even more rewarding. Given that metacognition requires a metacognitive reflective stance, there are opportunities for you to stop and reflect. As you read, I would encourage you to make a note of anything that you think might be useful, anything that you might want to consider implementing or doing differently in the future. There will be a reflective exercise at the end of the chapter to support you in gathering your thoughts and get the most use out of the chapter's ideas. Keeping notes of your emerging thoughts as you read through will help you with this. Jot down all your ideas; you can prioritise your next steps later on.

The more that you engage with these and your own questions, the more metacognitive skills you will employ and the more likely it is that you will get a lot out of the book. At the end of the chapter, take some time to reflect on and plan your next steps. Before moving on, here are some reflective questions.

What do you currently know about metacognition? Write some key ideas.

Why did you pick up this book?

Think about what you really want to get from this book. What are your priorities?

PART 1
Theory

2 Theoretical models

The learning process is fascinating. What really occurs within developing minds is a topic that has created a great deal of interest and for which there is a large amount of conjecture. This chapter looks at some of the theoretical processes and starts making the connections between what researchers have found and how this translates into practice. Research by Joyce and Showers (2002) showed that for adult learners to gain a deep understanding of new concepts, there is a need for exploration of its theoretical underpinnings. It offers the assurance that the approach is evidence based and increases the confidence of the learning practitioner. Therefore, this is where we begin – with theory. Throughout the book there is a heavy emphasis on the skill of reading, for, as we know, although initially we learn to read, we read to learn. School exams have exam papers that require reading and all subjects require note taking.

What is your theoretical knowledge of reading skill? Where would you position yourself in Figure 2.1?

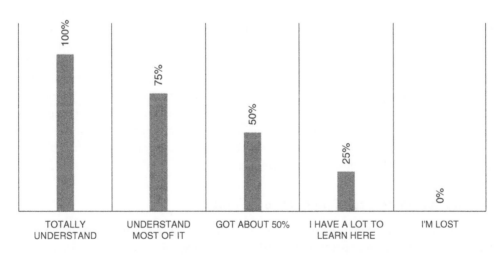

WHAT IS YOUR THEORETICAL KNOWLEDGE OF READING SKILL?

Figure 2.1 Self-reflective tool – what is your current theoretical knowledge of reading skill?

DOI: 10.4324/9781003315728-3

If we are concerned with general learning, why are we concentrating on reading?

Reading is fundamental to function effectively within society (Adams, 1994; Paris et al., 1983). Without reading skills, day-to-day activities (e.g., reading medicine bottles, warning signs, and maps) that many people take for granted may become a source of frustration, anger, and fear. Many jobs consider reading as a vital skill. Therefore, a person without good reading skills will be disadvantaged in many areas of modern life, potentially having a detrimental impact upon school attendance, school attainment, and employment status (Slavin, 1998). Furthermore, the Scottish Survey of Adult Literacy (SSAL) found that one of the key factors linked to lower literacy capabilities is poverty, with adults living in 15% of the most deprived areas in Scotland more likely to have literacy capabilities at the lower end of the scale (St. Clair et al., 2009). Similarly, US research (Kutner et al., 2007) found those with poorer literacy skills earn less, work in more routine occupations, are unemployed or economically inactive, live in more deprived areas, face health challenges, and have lower educational levels than others with better literacy skills.

The more we read, the better informed we are; therefore, readers are constantly upgrading their information and knowledge, facilitating greater understanding of the world around them (Adams, 1994). We go through a process of learning to read, so that ultimately, we can read to learn. Every exam paper, every school subject has at least some components that require reading and comprehension skills. It is also generally acknowledged that many successful reading strategies are also effective strategies for problem solving and evaluation skills across the curriculum (Clarke et al., 2013). These are especially useful skills when studying autonomously. Reading is important as all other subjects rely upon it, hence literacy learning has become the responsibility of all teachers through a process of literacy across learning within Scotland.

Why do we need to consider frameworks or models?

Everyone who teaches reading will have a guiding model of the reading process to which they refer to inform their instruction, whether or not they are aware of it. Models of reading are very useful as they help translate research into practice, detect where things may go wrong, and give us clues about which interventions might be the most appropriate (Ruddell & Unrau, 2004). Therefore, current models can provide crucial information about how to effectively teach within the classroom (Kintsch & Rawson, 2005). They provide a map of what is important within the teaching process. Also, if we know we are working with an evidence-based theoretical model in mind, it gives us something to refer to when deciding upon our children's learning plans. The earliest models of reading arose in the 1970s and as research has progressed, so too has their complexity and usefulness.

A historical understanding of reading models

The first models of reading can be classified as bottom-up models (with one example being from Gough (1972)). They describe the data-driven intake of stimulus in a process that develops to become automatic. An example of this is when you are sitting in the sun with your glass of wine reading a novel by your favorite author – the process is effortless. Everything you need comes from the pages. Yet, this approach was criticised because, as effortless as this may seem, on a sunny day with a blockbuster, the reader is still making use of contextual cues which require more than just letter stimulus to create meaning (Aaron et al., 1999; Ahmadi & Gilakjani, 2012). If we read the word, for example, cat, it takes more than the decoding of "c" "a" and "t" to relate the word to a fluffy little pet. Recognising the failings of a purely "bottom-up" based approach led to a second group of models classified as top-down models. Here, Goodman (1967) describes this process as a psycholinguistic guessing game where predictions are made and hypothesis are developed and tested. Here the reader would read "cat" and then refer to the text context and their experience of the world, which allows them to make meaning. The top-down process is described as starting with the experience of words and language, allowing us to recognise words and letters, having developed phonological awareness before aligning this with our existing knowledge of the world to create something meaningful.

Top-down models of the reading process describe a concept-driven approach where cues from the page, perhaps as context or graphic information, are used to create meaning through the activation of thinking and memory processes (Goodman, 1967).

However, top-down processes were later also criticised because skilled readers (or those reading something which is in line with their skill level) do not rely upon contextual or graphic cues (Adams, 1994; Ahmadi et al., 2013). When reading works, it is an automatic activity that places little demand on cognitive processes. Therefore, like the bottom-up reading process, purely top-down model explanations have fallen from favour.

There has thus been a move towards interactive models, which assume that bottom-up stimuli and top-down contextual information are complementary strategies which together support the creation of meaning in the most efficient way possible. The level of skill that the reader has, the type of text, and the goals of reading will all play a part in deciding the degree to which top-down and bottom-up processes are used.

The number and diversity of interactive models are vast; therefore, this chapter will concentrate on prominent and dynamic models which incorporate social, metacognitive, and motivational factors. These will be Transactional Theory, Schema Theory, Dual Coding Theory, Attitude-Influence Model, and Sociocognitive Theory.

Interactive, metacognitive, and sociocultural reading models

Transactional theory

Rosenblatt's model, Transactional Theory (1978), was one of the first to highlight the difference in process between reading nonfiction and fiction texts. She describes two alternative states of attention: efferent and aesthetic. The reader will quickly decide which of these stances to take once they begin reading. The efferent state is associated with nonfiction; here the goal of reading is to extract information from the text efficiently. Reading nonfiction is purposeful, with the focus being outside the reader, who hopes to gain information that will be useful after the reading session.

In contrast, the aesthetic state is associated with fiction and reading for enjoyment. Here, the emphasis is placed on online/live reading. This is a creative process that brings together the cues on the page with the reader's stream of thoughts and feelings; also regarded as the environment of engagement. The text becomes understood through the dynamic transaction, interaction, and relationship created between the reader and the text. As so much of the individual's thoughts and feelings are evident in this process, it is likely that individuals may interpret the same piece of text in completely different ways. Here, meaning is developed through reading and creating interpretations within the mind, rather than comprehension being merely a product of the text.

The implications of the Transactional model for the classroom are that, since fiction and nonfiction texts exist for different purposes (reading for information or reading for enjoyment), instruction around the reading of each piece of text needs to be suitable. If a child has read a piece of fiction, which elicits the aesthetic state of creatively reading for immersion and pleasure, and is then asked fact-based, memory-driven questions, it is likely to reduce enjoyment and motivation to read. More suitable questions for fiction texts would aim to encourage the exploration of the text in a creative and flexible way. Alternatively, fact-based questions are more suitable for nonfiction prose.

Children "read to learn" through nonfiction books and they need to be shown how to tackle functional reading which should be introduced from around the end of Year 1 in England and Wales or the equivalent Primary 2 in Scotland. Research shows that teachers working with groups of 6-8 children, each with a copy of the text and interacting and discussing the text, develops children's understanding and their ability to reflect.

Schema theory

A schema is an organised knowledge of the world (Anderson, 2004). Schema theory describes how this knowledge is integrated with information on the written page in order to add depth and understanding. The following sentence is used to exemplify the need for schema information:

"From walking in parallel system, the leader changes to cross system before leading the follower into the cross."

It is difficult to make sense of this sentence unless you have an Argentine Tango schema. Bransford and Johnson's (1972) research shows the importance of cues and prior knowledge for when participants are given a "trick" passage either on its own, with a supporting illustration, or with a related but less supportive illustration. Sense could only be made of their passage if provided with the cue of the supportive illustration. They found the level of comprehension affects the amount that readers would remember. Learners will only remember what they understand, an important thing to remember when teaching children and young people. Have we checked that they understand? How could we check that they really understand? If we use this example of the Argentine Tango, a person who takes tango lessons will understand and therefore retain more than a person who does not have similar prior knowledge of the dance.

In addition, the amount/type of pre-reading subject knowledge that the reader has directly affects the type of information that will be kept. For example, Chiesi et al. (1979) found that in a passage about baseball, those with high knowledge of the sport remembered more information about the strategic play, while those with low baseball knowledge remembered more incidental information. The same lesson cannot be equally accessed by all students, a point that is particularly relevant when teaching a class with diverse socioeconomic status.

Clearly, the level of background knowledge that we have impacts our understanding. Therefore, care needs to be taken in reading comprehension instruction (and assessment) to ensure that fixed answers are not culturally biased, as different cultures can offer very different answers based upon their own prior knowledge (Anderson, 2004). A schema is our "world knowledge" and everyone's "world knowledge" of different topics will be different. This plays a huge part in how we understand what we are learning and remembering, but also in the physical process of reading. For example, it takes longer to read about subjects we are less familiar with as there are fewer schemas (or less "world knowledge") to offer clues to support our understanding.

Anderson (2004) described six functions that the schemata serves:

- Additional scaffolding, for example, our schema of crime novels, ensures we infer there will be a criminal.
- Schemata provides a structure from which we can decide what is the most important information.
- The most important information is more easily identified; creating summaries or edits becomes easier.
- They help us elaborate upon the written words, allowing the reader to create pictures in their mind that go beyond the literal information on the page.
- The structure of our schema supports our memories, as we can methodically work through formats that cue recollections.
- This structure also allows us to question or hypothesise what else could happen in the text.

Schema theory has been very influential in best practice teaching approaches, as it demonstrates the importance of activating relevant knowledge prior to learning. From a culturally equitable perspective, schema theory also illustrates that prior knowledge should never be presumed. To maximise children's learning and understanding (and to equal the playing field of children's learning opportunities), topic-specific vocabulary needs to be taught explicitly. It is likely that even within a class of children from similar sub-cultural backgrounds, many children may not have had experiences that could be taken for granted in mass-produced reading materials. In addition, when teaching children of varying socioeconomic backgrounds, there is potential for unintentional discrimination within the group. New ideas are not equally accessible to all children, regardless of their decoding skills.

Schemas also provide valuable scaffolding that helps us make inferences which are important in the development of a coherent understanding of text. There are two overarching types of inference, of which the first is "text connecting" where local information is needed to connect information from different parts of the text. An example here might be: "Liz took a sandwich from her bag. It was tasty". Here we can infer that the sandwich was tasty. The second is "gap-filling" where global information is required to make sense of the information. For example: "Gill stood in the dock and waited for the judge". We can infer from our knowledge that Gill is in court and not at a harbour.

However, although inference making is critical to understanding, research indicates that not all readers make inferences, which results in shallow reading. The brain tries to work as efficiently as possible and inference making can be a costly cognitive process. The brain tries to decide what are necessary inferences; those required to understand text. Any additional benefits gained through elaborating information via superfluous inference, is not sufficiently economical. However, poor readers rarely make inferences, even when necessary for understanding.

Supporting the unskilled or developing learner to make more inferences can be achieved through asking and answering questions about the text, which promotes a deeper understanding.

Yet, while comprehension needs inferences, inferences need knowledge; therefore, comprehension needs knowledge. Research into schemas has led to various effective interventions including; previewing, "preparing your mind" and pre-reading vocabulary checks which will be discussed in Part 2.

Dual Coding Theory

Dual Coding Theory is a general theory of cognition that has been used to describe a variety of phenomena, of which reading is one. It brings together psychological and philosophical paradigms, and has been regarded as controversial in its alignment of visual and sensual input (Sadoski, 2008). It describes how, as information is inputted into the brain, it is characterised into two separate (although intertwined) cognitive codes, each recording separate characteristics. These are linguistic codes, those concerned with language, and non-linguistic codes, those concerned with imaginary. The latter type absorbs various sensory sources of information to transform it into a mental image. This dual nature allows for the synthesis of information with memories and prior knowledge. This has led to studies exploring the use of imagining images while reading text and these have proved that teaching children to visualise during the reading process promotes comprehension (Sadoski & Willson, 2006; Schirmer, 1995).

Attitude Influence Model

Mathewson's Model of Attitude Influence (2004) took a tricomponent template of attitude recognising:

1.   An affective component - the feelings surrounding reading.
2.   A conative component - the action readiness.
3.   A cognitive component - the evaluation of beliefs.

Factors which influence these levels of attitude before reading are:

*   cornerstone concepts (personal values, goals, etc.);
*   persuasive communication (which could be an encouraging teacher or an attractive-looking book);
*   cognitive feedback (where various factors are evaluated, including satisfaction of the ideas, external motivators, and internal feelings); and
*   affective feedback (specific feelings stimulated by the ideas and satisfaction with affect during reading).

All these aspects influence whether reading will take place. Each has several underpinning factors; for example, how the reader feels about reading will be influenced by their sense of mastery (for each aspect of reading, including decoding, vocabulary, fluency, and comprehension) or their experiences of reading. If the reader does not understand the word they are reading (vocabulary) or has insufficient decoding skills, they are unlikely to read. Similarly, if they have had an experience where reading aloud caused humiliation, they are unlikely to read.

While these aspects influence the intention to read, the intention to read affects behaviour (to read or not to read). This action can change as the process of reading takes place (e.g., losing focus when the text becomes overly complex).

This model highlights the importance of affective issues in teaching reading. For example, a child who has no interest in the topic will have reduced prevailing feelings about reading and, therefore, a poor intention to read. This could then prevent opportunities to practise reading, reducing their perceived ability and therefore compounding the lack of intention to read. In cases like this, the reader is less likely to employ fix-up strategies when reading breaks down because they are not invested in the subject (García-Rodicio & Sánchez, 2014).

There is wide agreement that there are two types of motivation: task-mastery orientation and performance orientation (Nicholls et al., 1989). The former is concerned with how people seek to improve their skills and accept new challenges, often referred to as intrinsic motivation. This is driven by factors internal to the individuals: they want to meet their personal goals rather than to oblige others (Nicholls et al., 1989). The latter is driven by the desire to maximise favourable evaluations, often known as extrinsic or surface motivation. This is driven by forces external to the self; for instance, pressure, punishment, and rewards that guide the individual to do things differently. Research shows that this is the less beneficial way of enhancing long-term performance.

We also refer to our judgement of our capabilities as self-efficacy; which is highly linked to reading motivation (Bandura, 1976; Law, 2009). If the individual has a sense of self-efficacy, they will see new reading material as a challenge; therefore, they will use their cognitive capabilities and become active readers with the goal of comprehending text (Pressley, Goodchild et al., 1989). However, to ensure motivation, the challenge should be moderate, not excessive, for otherwise the reader will give up (Rellinger et al., 1995). The reader requires a sense of competency that they can read - a sense that the prose is at an appropriate level of difficulty - in order to have sufficient motivation to invest time in reading (Pressley, Goodchild et al.,1989). This is the case when a child is given a book that is too easy, just as much as if the book they are given is too difficult.

Sociocognitive model

The Sociocognitive model is more complex than previous models as it acknowledges not only the text and the reader but also the context of the classroom (with a teacher), to recognise the social nature of reading. Here, the Sociocognitive Model by Ruddell and Unrau (2004) is a metaphor for the reading process. It incorporates three factors which work together in a unique and dynamic process: (1) reader, (2) teacher, and (3) text/environment.

(1)   The Reader

The learner has experiences of the world which have shaped their knowledge, under-standing, and beliefs. This unique information can be subdivided into affective con-ditions which include attitude, motivation, and sociocultural beliefs and values and their cognitive conditions which include declarative (knowledge of "what"), procedural (knowledge of "how") and conditional (knowledge of "when" and "why"). Together, they provide knowledge of language, text decoding strategies, metacognitive strategies, knowledge of the classroom, social interaction, and person/world knowledge. These reader characteristics influence how they interpret the information on the page and the meaning that they make of text in a process called "knowledge use and control". The meaning is shaped by how they construct this information based on their reading goals and purpose. This is an exclusive process, for what one reader brings to the expe-rience will be different from others. During the reading process, the reader allocates their comprehension and monitoring skills based on their prior knowledge, values, and beliefs. They predict and guess what the text means based upon the synthesis of all the information they have to hand to come to conclusions around meaning. Sometimes these conclusions will be in line with the author's while other times there will be differ-ences. Upon finishing the reading, the reader may then update their beliefs, attitudes, values, or knowledge. If the reader does not understand the text, they may attribute the breakdown in understanding to their own reader skills or alternatively attribute it to a fault of the text.

Throughout the reading process, tracking understanding of the text is key. These skills are called comprehension monitoring skills. If comprehension fails, the reader will have to employ some sort of fix-up strategies, for example, rereading to help repair the breakdown in comprehension. However, sometimes a reader will fail to recognise that comprehension has broken down and continue to decode text. Yet, the metacognitive reader will recognise when comprehension has failed and will try to regain meaning (Moore, 1983). However, much research has shown that developing or early readers tend not to employ fix-up strategies as they are overly concerned with decoding text (Baker, 1994; García-Rodicio & Sánchez, 2014).

The young reader's metacognitive skills develop. Real reading is about more than just decoding; it relies on the ability to think about what is being read, make a decision to take action, and employ that action. Without the use of these metacognitive strategies, coherent reading would be impossible (Ahmadi et al., 2013). However, the phenomenon becomes more complex as we recognise that comprehension monitoring or "fix-up" strategies are needed for effective reading (Dabarera et al., 2014). The fact that the reader has learned such a strategy and notices that text meaning is lost does not neces-sarily mean that the fix-up strategy will be employed (García-Rodicio & Sánchez, 2014). A reader will not search for meaning if they have no motivation to do so. Therefore, comprehension monitoring and metacognitive strategies more generally are closely linked with self-regulation and motivation (Souvignier & Mokhlesgerami, 2006). This link is reciprocal, as developing comprehension monitoring skills also enhances motivation for reading.

(2) The Teacher

The teacher is similarly unique and will have their own philosophies, values, beliefs, and understandings of effective teaching practices. Every teacher will have their own style, what they regard as important to teach and it is teachers' prior understanding of the world which will inform what teaching should look like in practice, what activities are important, what are the aspects of a task which need to be more carefully explained. Similar to the reader, it is the teacher's "executive and monitor" which dictates what they will give attention to and mediate within an optimum learning environment. Feedback that the teacher gets within a plenary session or their ongoing assessment of learning situations will inform the teacher's ever growing knowledge, beliefs, and values. To teach anything, it is necessary for the teacher to have knowledge of the subject, interest in the subject, and self-efficacy in teaching the subject.

The teacher is responsible for supporting the learner to make meaning, and this requires the creation of the optimum socially mediated environment (Gersten et al., 2001). If the teacher is in tune with the pupil's attributes and adapts their instruction to suit the child, being in tune with the child's stance, this will enhance their levels of motivation and comprehension. It is also essential to create a safe environment where children can discuss texts without fear of failure, creating a culture where it is good to seek verification and offer unique understandings instead of conforming to one teacher's perceptions of the "correct" answer.

The teacher would know the individual reader brings their own knowledge, beliefs, values, and attitudes to the reading process. Topic exploration with the teacher through collaborative discussion prior to reading will have a profound impact on the ease and depth of understanding, as well as motivation for engagement (Dowhower & Speidel, 1988). Greater engagement, in turn, leads to better memory retention of the information read. Conversation develops meaning and enables the development of metacognitive strategies (Pressley, Johnson et al., 1989) such as rereading (Haller et al., 1988) and comprehension monitoring (Dabarera et al., 2014; Payne & Manning, 1992). Class/teacher discussions support all to update and re-evaluate meaning and recognise the various rich interpretations, creating an inclusive classroom. The skills of questioning, cognitive challenging, re-evaluation, and creating meaning can transcend the contexts of literacy instruction, allowing construction of meaning across learning contexts. The outcomes for the reflective teacher (or metacognitively aware teacher) in this dialogical approach include a variety of thoughts of their teaching practices, or new knowledge or values (Gillies et al., 2011). This, in turn, will inform their ongoing practice.

With all this in mind, it is interesting that Swanson's (2008) synthesis of 26 studies of classroom observations of teacher behaviour concluded that little comprehension instruction took place. This was further explored by Ness (2009), who stated that this was influenced by a lack of teacher confidence in strategy instruction. Even now, some teacher training courses allow for little time to consider how to directly teach the skills needed to understand. The importance of teaching strategies needs to be highlighted and support provided to teachers to ensure they feel effective at doing so.

(3) The Text/Environment

The third component is the text/environment. Independent of ability, a child who has been exposed to reading will greatly influence their level of reading skill. So too will the number of different authors that a person is familiar with (Britton & Graesser, 1996). Choice of reading material, with an emphasis placed on reading for pleasure, is highly important. To get children motivated to read, they need to be reading something that interests them (Brookes, 2013). Furthermore, social opportunities like book discussions that enable joint engagement through interactions with others to discuss and explore interesting texts create an exciting curriculum (Ellis et al., 2014).

The unique relationships between the three components of teacher, environment, and student ultimately come together to determine the quality of the learning experience. When the three aspects align the learner's motivation and the teacher's work satisfaction, both accelerate and learning is a positive experience for all. This model builds upon previous models and acknowledges the potential impact of the quality of the teacher's lesson, which bears on individuals' motivation (Ruddell & Unrau, 2004). Also, the structure of the classroom or learning environment influences the developing reader's sense of ownership of their learning process. In turn, learning conversations and class discussions develop pupil/teacher relationships, enhancing trust and leading to a negotiation of meaning (Davies et al., 2013; Ruddell & Unrau, 2004).

Summary of reading models

In general, models have become increasingly complex (Moir, 2019). They emphasise the importance of effective interactions within classrooms as the teacher mediates meaning through discussion and comparison of ideas.

These models attempt to explain what good instruction is and how its application improves developing readers' skills. An important aspect is motivation, for a learner will only engage if motivated to do so. However, teachers are in a prime position to influence and instil motivation. Teachers not only come equipped with skills for teaching children, but also continually adapt their approaches, tailoring them to individuals, as and when necessary, in order to fully engage. This is all about pedagogy. Not what you teach but how you teach it.

Increasingly, we are seeing a paradigm shift away from assessment of children, in order to categorise their skill, towards assessment that informs the teacher. Here, the reflective or metacognitive teacher uses information of the child's learning to develop and adapt their teaching style to better scaffold and support the learner. The teacher can develop an understanding of the pupil's ability through a variety of ongoing assessment information, for example, discussion, written responses, interpretation of text, and knowledge acquisition.

Self-reflection tool

Having read the chapter, what is your theoretical knowledge of reading skill? Where would you position yourself in Figure 2.2? How different is this to how you assessed yourself in Figure 2.1?

WHAT IS YOUR THEORETICAL
KNOWLEDGE OF READING SKILL?

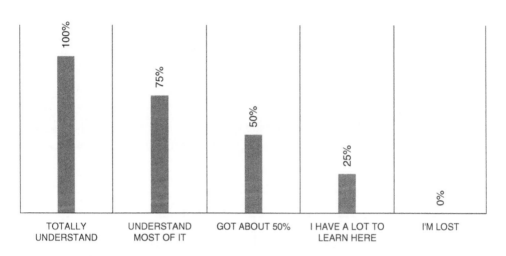

Figure 2.2 Self-reflective tool – what is your theoretical knowledge of reading skill after reading this chapter?

How might elements of the transactional model be seen in practice?

How might elements of the schematic model be seen in practice?

How might elements of the dual coding model be seen in practice?

How might elements of the attitude influence model be seen in practice?

How might elements of the sociocognitive model be seen in practice?

Which is your favourite model and why?

Once you have thought about these questions, identify one or two areas that you want to enhance. How are you going to do this? What is the easiest way for you to measure your impact?

What am I going to try?	How can I measure impact?

Figure 2.3 Chapter planning tool

You can always come back to this chapter to build upon other areas of practice; however, it is better to keep it simple and easy to manage changes by only committing to one or two at a time.

References

Aaron, P. G., Joshi, M., & Williams, K. A. (1999). Not all reading disabilities are alike. *Journal of Learning Disabilities, 32*(2), 120-137.

Adams, M. J. (1994). *Beginning to read: Thinking and learning about print*. MIT Press.

Ahmadi, M. R., & Gilakjani, A. P. (2012). Reciprocal teaching strategies and their impacts on English reading comprehension. *Theory and Practice in Language Studies, 2*(10), 2053.

Ahmadi, M. R., Ismail, H. N., & Abdullah, M. K. K. (2013). The importance of metacognitive reading strategy awareness in reading comprehension. *English Language Teaching, 6*(10), 235.

Anderson, R. (2004). Role of the reader's schema in comprehension, learning and memory. In R. Ruddell & N. Unrau (Eds.), *Theoretical models and processes of reading* (5th ed., pp. 594-606). International Reading Association.

Baker, L. (1994). Fostering metacognitive development. *Advances in Child Development and Behavior, 25*, 201-239.

Bandura, A. (1976). Self-reinforcement: Theoretical and methodological considerations. *Behaviorism, 4*(2), 135-155.

Bransford, J., & Johnson, M. (1972). Contextual prerequisites for understanding: Some investigations of comprehension and recall. *Journal of Verbal Learning and Verbal Behavior, 11*(6), 717-726.

Britton, B., & Graesser, A. (1996). *Models of understanding text*. Lawrence Erlbaum Associates.

Brookes, G. (2013). *What works for children and young people with literacy difficulties*? The effectiveness of intervention schemes. www.interventionsforliteracy.org.uk/widgets_GregBrooks/What_works_for_children_fourth_ed.pdf

Chiesi, H., Spilich, G., & Voss, J. (1979). Acquisition of domain-related information in relation to high and low domain knowledge. *Journal of Verbal Learning and Verbal Behavior, 18*(3), 257-273.

Clarke, P. J., Truelove, E., Hulme, C., & Snowling, M. J. (2013). *Developing reading comprehension*. John Wiley & Sons.

Dabarera, C., Renandya, W. A., & Zhang, L. J. (2014). The impact of metacognitive scaffolding and monitoring on reading comprehension. *System, 42*, 462-473.

Davies, D., Jindal - Snape, D., Collier, C., Digby, R., Hay, P., & Howe, A. (2013). Creative learning environments in Education - A systematic literature review. *Thinking Skills and Creativity, 8*, 80-91.

Dowhower, S., & Speidel, G. (1988). Let's teach unskilled readers like skilled readers: A closer look at meaning-based instruction. *Reading Research and Instruction, 28*(2), 50-60.

Ellis, A., Denton, D., & Bond, J. (2014). An analysis of research on metacognitive teaching strategies. *Procedia - Social and Behavioral Sciences, 116*, 4015-4024.

García-Rodicio, H., & Sánchez, E. (2014). Does the detection of misunderstanding lead to its revision? *Metacognition and Learning, 9*(3), 265-286.

Gersten, R., Fuchs, L. S., Williams, J. P., & Baker, S. (2001). Teaching reading comprehension strategies to students with learning disabilities: A review of research. *Review of Educational Research, 71*(2), 279-320.

Gillies, R., Nichols, K., & Burgh, G. (2011). Promoting problem-solving and reasoning during cooperative inquiry science. *Teaching Education, 22*(4), 427-443.

Goodman, K. (1967). Reading: A psycholinguistic guessing game. *Journal of the Reading Specialist, 6*(4), 126-135.

Gough, P. (1972). One second of reading. *Visible Language, 6*(4), 291-320.

Haller, E., Child, D., & Walberg, H. (1988). Can comprehension be taught? A quantitative synthesis of "metacognitive" studies. *Educational Researcher, 17*(9), 5-8.

Joyce, B., & Showers, B. (2002). Student achievement through staff development. In B. Joyce & B. Showers (Eds.), *Designing training and peer coaching: Out needs for learning*. National College for School Leadership.

Kintsch, W., & Rawson, K. (2005). Comprehension. In M. Snowling & C. Hulme (Eds.), *The science of reading* (pp. 209-226). Blackwell.

Kutner, M., Greenberg, E., Jin, Y., Boyle, B., Hsu, Y. C., & Dunleavy, E. (2007). *Literacy in Everyday Life: Results from the 2003 National Assessment of Adult Literacy*. NCES 2007-490. National Center for Education Statistics.

Law, Y.-K. (2009). The role of attribution beliefs, motivation and strategy use in Chinese fifth-graders' reading comprehension. *Educational Research, 51*(1), 77-95.

Mathewson, G. (2004). Model of attitude influence upon reading and learning to read. In R. Ruddell & N. Unrau (Eds.), *Theoretical models and processes of reading* (pp. 1431-1461). International Reading Association.

Moir, T. (2019). The psychology within models of reading comprehension and the educational psychologist's role in taking theory into practice. *Educational and Child Psychology, 36*(3), 52-64.

Moore, P. J. (1983). Aspects of metacognitive knowledge about reading. *Journal of Research in Reading, 6*(2), 87-102.

Ness, M. (2009). Reading comprehension strategies in secondary content area classrooms: Teacher use of and attitudes towards reading comprehension instruction. *Reading Horizons, 49*(2), 143-166.

Nicholls, J. G., Cheung, P. C., Lauer, J., & Patashnick, M. (1989). Individual differences in academic motivation: Perceived ability, goals, beliefs, and values. *Learning and Individual Differences, 1*(1), 63-84.

Paris, S., Lipson, M., & Wixson, K. (1983). Becoming a strategic reader. *Contemporary Educational Psychology, 8*(3), 293-316.

Payne, B., & Manning, B. (1992). Basal reader instruction: Effects of comprehension monitoring training on reading comprehension, strategy use and attitude. *Reading Research and Instruction, 32*(1), 29-38.

Pressley, M., Goodchild, F., Fleet, J., Zajchowski, R., & Evans, E. D. (1989). The challenges of classroom strategy instruction. *The Elementary School Journal, 89*(3), 301-342.

Pressley, M., Johnson, C., Symons, S., McGoldrick, J., & Kurita, J. (1989). Strategies that improve children's memory and comprehension of text. *The Elementary School Journal, 90*(1), 3.

Rellinger, E., Borkowski, J. G., Turner, L. A., & Hale, C. A. (1995). Perceived task difficulty and intelligence: Determinants of strategy use and recall. *Intelligence, 20*(2), 125-143.

Rosenblatt, L. (1978). *The reader, the text, the poem the transactional theory of the literary work*. Southern Illinois University Press.

Ruddell, R., & Unrau, N. (2004). Sociocognitive model of reading. In R. Ruddell & N. Unrau (Eds.), *Theoretical models and processes of reading* (pp. 1462-1523). International Reading Association.

Sadoski, M. (2008). Dual coding theory: Reading comprehension and beyond. In C. Block & S. Parris (Eds.), *Comprehension instruction: Research-based best practices* (Vol. 2, pp. 38-49). New York: Guilford Press.

Sadoski, M., & Willson, V. (2006). Effects of a theoretically based large-scale reading intervention in a multicultural urban school district. *American Educational Research Journal, 43*(1), 137-154.

Schirmer, B. (1995). Mental imagery and the reading comprehension of deaf children. *Reading Research and Instruction, 34*(3), 177-189.

Slavin, R. E. (1998). Reading by nine: What will it take? *Peabody Journal of Education, 73*(3-4), 68-80.

Souvignier, E., & Mokhlesgerami, J. (2006). Using self-regulation as a framework for implementing strategy instruction to foster reading comprehension. *Learning and Instruction, 16*(1), 57-71.

St. Clair, R., Maclachlan, K., & Tett, L. (2009). Educational entrepreneurs? Practitioner-led action research and the formation of the professional adult literacies instructor. *Studies in the Education of Adults, 41*(2), 175-191.

Swanson, E. (2008). Observing reading instruction for students with learning disabilities: A synthesis. *Learning Disability Quarterly, 31*(3), 115-133.

3 Research into strategy instruction

This chapter is going to continue using our reading example to illustrate how the research has informed our need to explicitly teach strategies.

How much do you know about the research related to strategies in learning? Where would you position yourself in Figure 3.1?

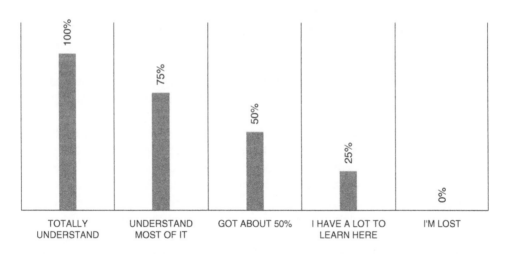

HOW MUCH DO YOU KNOW ABOUT THE RESEARCH RELATED TO STRATEGIES IN LEARNING?

Figure 3.1 Self-reflective tool – what is your current understanding of the research into strategies?

Why teach strategies?

The importance of teaching comprehension strategies was not acknowledged until Durkin undertook classroom observations in 1978. His studies illustrated that, while comprehension was regularly assessed within the classroom, there was no evidence of its tuition. Further studies confirmed that little strategy instruction took place even though research showed that children benefit from explicit instruction (Morrow et al., 1997), especially those with lower reading

DOI: 10.4324/9781003315728-4

skills (Brown et al., 1996; Duffy et al., 1987). Research also showed that even if children had missed out on comprehension strategy instruction when young, they would still benefit from strategy instruction later in life (Edmonds et al., 2009). Indeed, it is never too late. It is generally now recognised that appropriate comprehension strategies need to be effectively taught (Bensley & Spero, 2014; Morrow et al., 1997). Yet, while there has been an increase in programmes targeted towards effective strategy instruction, there continues to be little evidence to suggest they are taught explicitly (Parker & Hurry, 2007; Moir, Boyle & Woolfson, 2020).

The definition of comprehension strategies

Comprehension strategies are defined by McKeown and Isabel (2009) as a "routine that represents a specific mental processing action that is part of a complex process executed towards a goal such as understanding what one has read". Comprehension strategies have also been defined as being a conscious, planned set of steps that excellent readers use to make sense of text.

Early research into what successful instruction looked like concentrated on measuring the effectiveness of discrete approaches within the classroom. These studies confirmed the impact of strategies, including, for example, mental imagery and its links with the Dual Coding Theory (Horowitz-Kraus et al., 2013) (see Chapter 2) and particular cognitive strategies, for example, summarisation (Brown & Day, 1983), structure (Taylor & Beach, 1984), and organising data (Gardner, 1986).

Other research has looked at adult readers with no specific training to identify the strategies most likely to be used intuitively. For example, McNamara (2004) found that the most likely used strategy was paraphrasing, followed by bridging, while the least likely was prediction. What was also interesting within this study was that different results were found when different types of text were being used; therefore, strategy use was not only dependent on the reader's ability. This supported the models mentioned in Chapter 2, particularly Transactional Theory and the Sociocognitive Model.

This area of research has been far from straightforward, for what constitutes a strategy has altered significantly over time. In 1978-2000, 45 strategies were proposed (Block & Duffy, 2008), yet since 2000 these 45 approaches have been combined into nine strategies. Indeed, what constitutes a strategy or a skill has added complexity to a complex issue (Harris et al., 2008).

There are limitations within the research. For example, there was and is a wide variation in the participant ages studied or the definitions of learning abilities/disabilities which impacts upon meta-analysis findings (Davis, 2010). Also, published studies rarely provide further information on effect sizes of pre and post comparisons and treatment control. In addition, the measure that studies use varies. Across the body of research, researcher-developed tools show greater impact than standardised tools (Davis, 2010). This is perhaps because when researchers develop their own assessment tools, the measures will be designed to measure the aspect of reading that the intervention is targeting. Yet, norm-referenced or standardised cognitive tests will measure more general skills. Therefore, the latter approach takes a broader look at the transference and generalisation of an intervention.

Making comparisons using effect sizes

Fewer studies have taken place to make sense of reading comprehension than other reading skills, such as decoding or vocabulary. However, there is enough evidence for findings from various studies to be pulled together into a synthesis or metaanalysis so that sense can be made of the overarching findings. Through use of the scale known as effect size (ES), different instructional approaches can be reliably compared to each other using the measurement *d*. The greater the effect size, the more effective the approach. In 1988, Cohen's research indicated that a small, average, and large effect size could be considered 0.2, 0.4, and 0.6, respectively. However, John Hattie's study in 2008 of 800 studies related to achievement showed that the average effect size of an intervention was 0.4. Therefore, it is now generally regarded that any effect size smaller than 0.4 perhaps requires very careful consideration before implementation (Hattie, 2008). Interventions with effect sizes 0.4-0.6 could be considered above average and those with effect sizes of 0.6 or more are considered excellent.

Synthesises of reading comprehension research

One of the first syntheses of comprehension strategies took place in 1988 by Haller et al. They reviewed 20 studies which suggested an average effect size (ES[1]) of *d* = 0.71 for 26 instructional techniques, including self-questioning and raising awareness of textual inconsistency, monitoring, and regulation strategies. However, further research was needed to differentiate the effectiveness of these strategies.

Mastropieri and Scruggs (1997) found in their study that questioning led by the teacher had the greatest impact in promoting comprehension. This yielded an ES of *d* = 1.33 which could be favourably compared with text enhancement (that is the use of illustrations, spatial organisations, and adjunct aids) (*d* = 0.92) and skill training/reinforcement (*d* = 0.62), which included direct instruction or repeated readings strategies. Using graphics was later supported by qualitative research in 2013 by Brenna and Jaeger and Wiley in 2014.

Sencibaugh's 2007 synthesis found 15 studies conducted between 1985 and 2005 which met their criteria of reading comprehension intervention studies for children with an identified learning disability. They categorised the approaches related to how dependent they were on "auditory or language strategies" or "visually dependent strategies". They found that the former was more effective than the latter, with effect sizes being *d* = 1.18 compared with *d* = 0.94, respectively.

Swanson (1999) reviewed 92 studies undertaken between 1963 and 1997 in their meta-analysis on reading instruction with children with learning difficulties. Cognitive and direct instruction approaches proved to be most effective (*d* = 1.15) compared with strategy instruction alone (*d* = 0.98). Researcher-designed measures (*d* = 0.81) showed greater impact than standardised measures (*d* = 0.45). The most effective strategies included direct questioning, modelling by the teacher, strategy cues, and elaboration through the provision of concepts, explanations, steps, or procedures.

In 2010, Berkeley et al. also undertook a meta-analysis of interventions and studies from 1995-2006 for children with learning disabilities including those with dyslexia or those categorised as "reading disabled". This included 40 studies, and it was found that instruction had a beneficial impact when measuring with both norm-referenced tests (*d* = 0.52) and other measures (*d* = 0.70). This analysis confirms many of the most effective approaches, including questioning/strategy instruction (*d* = 0.75) and text enhancements (*d* = 0.61). It also highlighted some ineffective approaches, including perceptual training (*d* = 0.08) and modality training (*d* = 0.14). Importantly, congruent with Parker and Hurry (2007), they highlighted that specialised strategy instruction is not generally taking place and that intervention implementation was an area for further research (see Chapter 11).

One of the largest literature review of reading practices was conducted by the *Eunice Kennedy Shriver*, National Institute of Child Health and Human Development (NICHD) (2000), comprising 100,000 studies looking at each of the five components of reading: phonemic awareness, phonics, fluency, vocabulary, and reading comprehension. While these components were considered separately, it was clear from their conclusions that reading is a complex task requiring interactivity between all five components – the sum of which is greater than its constituent parts. While the NICHD did not undertake a meta-analysis of reading comprehension approaches (because of the small number of studies), they could conclude that for comprehension to develop, the following was true:

- Linking phonemic awareness to letters makes learning more efficient.
- Fluency was a factor required for comprehension and learners benefited from guided instruction.
- Vocabulary needed to be taught explicitly.
- Comprehension needed to be taught explicitly and six strategies were identified as effective:
  o Twenty-two studies explored comprehension monitoring, the ability to recognise when the reader understands the text.
  o Ten studies reported on cooperative learning, that is, when readers need to learn to work in groups, listen, and understand their peers as they read, and help one another to use strategies that promote effective reading comprehension and readers learn to focus and discuss reading materials.
  o Reported within 11 studies was the use of graphic and semantic organisers, including story maps which externally systematise information, aiding understanding.
  o Question-answering strategies were reported by 17 studies to help readers develop skills in answering questions and making inferences.
  o Question generation was reported in 27 studies as a strategy for readers to develop their ability to generate questions or inferences.
  o Summarisation was reported within 18 studies as a strategy to develop the reader's understanding of key points within text.
  o In addition, many of these strategies have also been effectively used in the category of "multiple strategy" or Multiple Comprehension Strategy Instruction (MSCI) where readers and teachers interact with texts. Thirty-eight studies reported on various ways to coordinate several processes to construct meaning from texts. How instruction of a multiple strategy approach could be employed for the highest impact was an area for further research.

Block and Pressley (2007) categorised these strategies into one of four subgroups. Those are appropriate for:

1. Vocabulary comprehension.
2. Paragraph understanding.
3. Longer passage reading of seven or more pages.
4. Integration of the self with the wider world.

Problems defining strategies

While identification of these strategies has been influential, difficulties remain (Garner, 1987; Harris et al., 2008). For example, strategies were defined as a conscious, planned set of steps that excellent readers use to make sense of text. However, graphic organisers are perhaps better described as a technique and cooperative learning as a structured format for learning (McKeown & Isabel, 2009). Furthermore, comprehension monitoring is a complex term that perhaps merits greater consideration than a single strategy (Haller et al., 1988).

As can be seen, over time these individual strategies have been amalgamated into different manifestations, taking multiple strategy approaches, which are now generally regarded as more effective than the use of individual approaches. These multiple strategies are especially effective "where teachers and pupils interact over texts" (Gersten et al., 2001; Rosenshine & Meister, 1994).

Multiple strategy approaches

Many interventions have blended these aspects into approaches that develop children's reading comprehension and Moir et al.'s (2020) study investigated the efficacy of the different approaches. The inclusion criteria were:

- Studies are of sufficient sample size to determine a reliable effect size.
- The multiple strategy approach must take a universal approach to raise attainment for all, rather than only for a small sub-group (e.g., those identified with additional support needs).
- The approach must have multiple strategies.
- Other interventions which have been identified as beneficial for improving reading comprehension (including BRP Durham, Phono-Graphix, ARROWS, and paired reading (Brookes, 2013)), yet where comprehension was not the main or only focus of the intervention were not included.

Some were highly branded into widely established approaches, while others were lesser known to practitioners. The interventions included Reciprocal Teaching (RT) by Palincsar et al. (1987), Informed Strategies for Learning (ISL) by Paris et al. (1984), Think-Aloud Instruction (TAI) by Bereiter and Bird (1985), Collaborative Strategic Reading (CSR) by Vaughn et al. (2001), Transactional Strategies Instruction (TSI) by El-Dinary (2002), Peer-Assisted Learning Strategies (PALS) by Fuchs et al. (1997), Concept-Oriented Reading Instruction (CORI) by Guthrie et al. (2004) and Strathclyde Higher Order Thinking Skills (SHORS) by McCartney et al. (2015). The study showed that there was potential in taking forward the latter approach.

Strathclyde Higher Order Reading Skills programme (SHORS)

The SHORS programme takes its research principles from two studies: James-Burdumy et al. (2009) and Shanahan et al. (2010). The US Department of Education commissioned the large-scale James-Burdumy et al. (2009) study. Given that the evidence had previously cited multiple strategy reading comprehension approaches to yield bigger learning gains than when strategies were taught in isolation, their study was to assess which of four multiple strategy supplementary reading comprehension curricula interventions would show the largest gains. Data from children attending over 200 schools and 10 American districts were analysed. Using a variety of different measures, including observational, teacher, implementation, and test data, they evaluated four multiple strategy interventions. Surprisingly, the results showed that none of the interventions had a significant positive impact on student's reading comprehension.

What was even more surprising was that one approach had a statistically significant negative impact. Therefore, the mere act of putting together a package of strategies would not be enough to see a positive change. There needed to be other factors that, if in place, brought about increased reading comprehension. To find out, they undertook secondary analysis of the observational data. What they found was that when there was a positive impact on children's comprehension, there was explicit instruction, effective teacher management and responsiveness, and student engagement.

The second American study, which highlighted theoretical principles within the SHORs approach, was undertaken by Shanahan et al. (2010). This study looked at the existing body of research and was focused on teaching comprehension to young children from kindergarten (Primary 1 in Scotland and Reception in England and Wales) to Grade 3 (Primary 5 or Year 5 in England and Wales). Their sweep of papers found 812 studies on reading comprehension, of which only 27 met their inclusion criteria. From this, they made the following five recommendations:

- Teachers need to teach children how to use reading comprehension strategies, either individually or using a combination of research-based strategies. The teacher, being attuned to the children, will increase the child's responsibility for the independent use of a strategy at an appropriate pace as the reader's skill develops. They cited some strategies for which there was an existing evidence base. These were activating prior knowledge, questioning, visualising, monitoring, clarifying and fixing-up, drawing inferences, and summarising/retelling.
- Teachers teach students to identify and use the text's organisational structure to comprehend, learn, and remember content. The teacher also provided instruction for common structures and aimed to support children to make links between texts.
- Teachers would provide opportunities to support classroom discussions of quality which were related to the texts. The teacher would ask probing questions to enable students to gain a deeper understanding and guide students through focused, high-quality discussion on the meaning of text.
- Teachers select good quality materials from a variety of genres (Britton & Graesser, 1996).
- Teachers saw their role as one who established a positive and engaging learning environment which was conducive to motivating children to engage. They suggested offering pupils opportunities for discussion and a choice of reading materials. It was also encouraged that children would acknowledge the benefits of reading.

Shanahan et al. (2010) recognise that there is insufficient evidence to wholly invest in one of these five approaches to the exclusion of everything else. Therefore, they recommend a far more flexible approach which, when used, can be far easier to implement (Boyle et al., 2010) (see Chapter 11).

The SHORS intervention used in the McCartney et al. (2015) study took these underlying principles and designed the intervention around these aspects and showed that they had an impact on reading outcomes. The approach encourages a shift in practice instead of new cur-riculums or prescriptive lesson plans. It is a methodology that allows teachers to blend the approach with their teaching resources in entire class and group settings. McCartney et al. (2015) facilitated the training of teachers where they are encouraged to discuss its appli-cation within the classroom. This involvement creates ownership and potentially increased effectiveness (Moir, 2018).

Interestingly, the McCartney et al. (2015) study also compared the progress of children with language learning impairments and non-language learning impaired pupils and found that over a year their reading comprehension abilities improved with similar rapidity. It was regarded as a universal approach which could be easily implemented without costly resources. However, their study had no control and was an area for further research. Chapter 4 will dis-cuss how this research was then built upon by Moir et al. (2020).

Self-reflection tool

Having read the chapter, what is your understanding of the research into strategies after reading this chapter? Where would you position yourself in Figure 3.2? How different is this to how you assessed yourself in Figure 3.1?

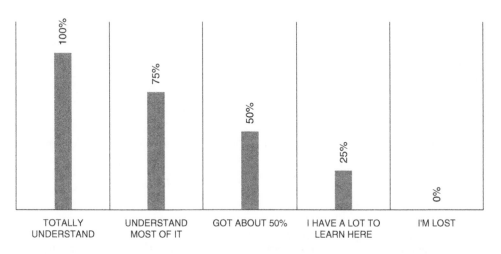

HOW MUCH DO YOU KNOW ABOUT THE RESEARCH RELATED TO STRATEGIES IN LEARNING?

| TOTALLY UNDERSTAND | UNDERSTAND MOST OF IT | GOT ABOUT 50% | I HAVE A LOT TO LEARN HERE | I'M LOST |

Figure 3.2 Self-reflective tool – what is your understanding of the research into strategies after reading this chapter?

How would you describe a strategy?

What do you think of the research findings in this chapter?

Can you see any links between the theories outlined in Chapter 2 and the research discussed here in Chapter 3?

Once you have thought about these questions, identify one or two areas that you want to enhance. How are you going to do this? What is the easiest way for you to measure your impact?

What am I going to try/read or do?	How can I measure impact?

Figure 3.3 Chapter planning tool

You can always come back to this chapter to build on other areas of practice; however, it is better to keep it simple and easy to manage changes by only committing to one or two at a time.

Note

1   Standardised effect sizes are being used as this allows all effect sizes to be put on the same scale using Cohen's *d*.

References

Bensley, A., & Spero, R. (2014). Improving critical thinking skills and metacognitive monitoring through direct infusion. *Thinking Skills and Creativity, 12,* 55-68.

Bereiter, C., & Bird, M. (1985). Use of thinking aloud in identification and teaching of reading comprehension strategies. *Cognition and Instruction, 2*(2), 131-156.

Berkeley, S., Scruggs, T. E., & Mastropieri, M. A. (2010). Reading comprehension instruction for students with learning disabilities, 1995-2006: A meta-analysis. *Remedial and Special Education, 31*(6), 423-436.

Block, C., & Duffy, G. (2008). Research on teaching comprehension. In C. C. Block & S. R. Parris (Eds.), *Comprehension instruction: Research-based best practices. Solving problems in the teaching of literacy* (Vol. 2, 2nd ed.). Guilford Press.

Block, C., & Pressley, M. (2007). Best practices in teaching comprehension. *Best Practices in Literacy Instruction, 3*, 220-242.

Boyle, J., McCartney, E., O' Hare, A., & Law, J. (2010). Intervention for receptive language disorder. *Developmental Medicine and Child Neurology, 52*(11), 994-999.

Brenna, B. (2013). How graphic novels support reading comprehension strategy development in children. *Literacy, 47*(2), 88-94.

Britton, B., & Graesser, A. (1996). *Models of understanding text*. Lawrence Erlbaum Associates.

Brookes, G. (2013). *What works for children and young people with literacy difficulties? The effectiveness of intervention schemes.* http://www.interventionsforliteracy.org.uk/widgets_GregBrooks/What_works_for_children_fourth_ed.pdf

Brown, A., & Day, J. (1983). Macrorules for summarizing texts: The development of expertise. *Journal of Verbal Learning and Verbal Behaviour, 22*(1), 1-14.

Brown, R., Pressley, M., Van Meter, P., & Schuder, T. (1996). A quasi-experimental validation of transactional strategies instruction with low-achieving second-grade readers. *Journal of Educational Psychology, 88*(1), 18-37.

Cohen, J. (1988). *Statistical power analysis for the behavioral sciences* (2nd ed.). Erlbaum.

Davis, D. (2010). *A meta-analysis of comprehension strategy instruction for upper elementary and middle school students* [Unpublished PhD dissertation, Vanderbilt University].

Duffy, G., Roehler, L., Sivan, E., Rackliffe, G., Book, C., Meloth, M., ... Bassiri, D. (1987). Effects of explaining the reasoning associated with using reading strategies. *Reading Research Quarterly, 22*(3), 347-368.

Durkin, D. (1978). What classroom observations reveal about reading comprehension instruction. *Reading Research Quarterly, 14*(4), 481-533.

Edmonds, M., Vaughn, S., Wexler, J., Reutebuch, C., Cable, A., Tackett, K. K., & Schnakenberg, J. W. (2009). A synthesis of reading interventions and effects on reading comprehension outcomes for older struggling readers. *Review of Educational Research, 79*(1), 262-300.

El-Dinary, P. (2002). Challenges of implementing transactional strategies instruction for reading comprehension. In C. Block & M. Pressley (Eds.), *Comprehension instruction: Research-based best practices* (pp. 201-215). Guilford Press.

Eunice Kennedy Shriver, National Institute of Child Health and Human Development (NICHD), NIH, HHS (2000). *National reading panel report: Teaching children to read*. www.nichd.nih.gov.

Fuchs, D., Fuchs, L., Mathes, P., & Simmons, D. (1997). Peer-assisted learning strategies: Making classrooms more responsive to diversity. *American Educational Research Journal, 34*(1), 174-206.

Gardner, K. (1986). *Reading in today's schools*. Oliver & Boyd.

Garner, R. (1987). *Metacognition and reading comprehension*. Ablex.

Gersten, R., Fuchs, L. S., Williams, J. P., & Baker, S. (2001). Teaching reading comprehension strategies to students with learning disabilities: A review of research. *Review of Educational Research, 71*(2), 279-320.

Guthrie, J., Wigfield, A., Barbosa, P., Perencevich, K., Taboada, A., Davis, M., ... Tonks, S. (2004). Increasing reading comprehension and engagement through concept-oriented reading instruction. *Journal of Educational Psychology, 96*(3), 403-423.

Haller, E., Child, D., & Walberg, H. (1988). Can comprehension be taught? A quantitative synthesis of "metacognitive" studies. *Educational Researcher, 17*(9), 5-8.

Harris, K., Alexander, P., & Graham, S. (2008). Michael Pressley's contributions to the history and future of strategies research. *Educational Psychologist, 43*(2), 86-96.

Hattie, J. (2008). The nature of evidence. In *Visible learning: A synthesis of over 800 meta-analyses relating to achievement*. Routledge.

Horowitz-Kraus, T., Vannest, J. J., & Holland, S. K. (2013). Overlapping neural circuitry for narrative comprehension and proficient reading in children and adolescents. *Neuropsychologia, 51*(13), 2651-2662.

Jaeger, A., & Wiley, J. (2014). Do illustrations help or harm metacomprehension accuracy? *Learning and Instruction, 34*, 58-73.

James-Burdumy, S., Mansfield, W., Deke, J., Carey, N., Lugo-Gil, J., Hershey, A., ... & Faddis, B. (2009). *Effectiveness of selected supplemental reading comprehension interventions: Impacts on a first cohort of fifth-grade students*. NCEE 2009-4032. National Center for Education Evaluation and Regional Assistance.

Mastropieri, M., & Scruggs, T. (1997). Best practices in promoting reading comprehension in students with learning disabilities: 1976 to 1996. *Remedial and Special Education, 18*(4), 197–214.

McCartney, E., Boyle, J., & Ellis, S. (2015). Developing a universal reading comprehension intervention for mainstream primary schools within areas of social deprivation for children with and without language-learning impairment: A feasibility study. *International Journal of Language & Communication Disorders, 50*(1), 129–135.

McKeown, M., & Isabel, B. (2009). The role of metacognition in reading comprehension. In D. Hacker, J. Dunlosky, & A. Graesser (Eds.), *Handbook of metacognition in education* (pp. 7–25). Routledge.

McNamara, D. (2004). SERT: Self-explanation reading training. *Discourse Processes, 38*(1), 1–30.

Moir, T. (2018). Why is implementation science important to intervention design and evaluation, within educational settings? In *Frontiers in education* (Vol. 3, p. 61). Frontiers.

Moir, T., Boyle, J., & Woolfson, L. M. (2020). Developing higher-order reading skills in mainstream primary schools: A metacognitive and self-regulatory approach. *British Educational Research Journal, 46*(2), 399–420.

Morrow, L. M., Pressley, M., Smith, J., & Smith, M. (1997). The effect of a literature-based program integrated into literacy and science instruction with children from diverse backgrounds. *Reading Research Quarterly, 32*(1), 54–76.

Palincsar, A., Brown, A., & Martin, S. (1987). Peer interaction in reading comprehension instruction. *Educational Psychologist, 22*(3–4), 231–253.

Paris, S. G., Cross, D. R., & Lipson, M. Y. (1984). Informed strategies for learning: A program to improve children's reading awareness and comprehension. *Journal of Educational Psychology, 76*(6), 1239–1252.

Parker, M., & Hurry, J. (2007). Teachers' use of questioning and modelling comprehension skills in primary classrooms. *Educational Review, 59*(3), 299–314.

Rosenshine, B., & Meister, C. (1994). Reciprocal reading: A review of the research. *Review of Educational Research, 64*(4), 479–530.

Sencibaugh, J. (2007). Meta-analysis of reading comprehension interventions for students with learning disabilities: Strategies and implications. *Reading Improvement, 44*(1), 6–22.

Shanahan, T., Callison, K., Carriere, C., Duke, N. K., Pearson, P. D., Schatschneider, C., & Torgesen, J. (2010b). *Improving reading comprehension in kindergarten through 3rd grade: IES practice guide*. NCEE 2010-4038. National Center for Education Evaluation and Regional Assistance (ED); What Works Clearinghouse (ED).

Swanson, H. (1999). Reading research for students with LD: A meta-analysis of intervention outcomes. *Journal of Learning Disabilities, 32*(6), 504–532.

Taylor, B., & Beach, R. (1984). The effects of text structure instruction on middle-grade students' comprehension and production of expository text. *Reading Research Quarterly, 19*(2), 134–146.

Vaughn, S., Klingner, J., & Bryant, D. (2001). Collaborative strategic reading as a means to enhance peer-mediated instruction for reading comprehension and content-area learning. *Remedial and Special Education, 22*(2), 66–74.

4 UK research

This chapter talks through how the strategies and approaches discussed in Chapter 3 were taken forward in a UK study. The purpose of the study was to build an effective evidence base and the purpose of the chapter is to demonstrate the effectiveness of the approaches discussed throughout the book. In this example, the study focus was to boost reading comprehension skills and therefore this was the primary evaluation tool. However, as the study findings show, the approaches were deemed effective across the curriculum. However, as has already been discussed, reading is the route to learning and comprehending text is essential for every subject.

How confident are you that what you do in school is evidence based? Where would you position yourself in Figure 4.1?

HOW CONFIDENT ARE YOU THAT WHAT YOU DO IN SCHOOL IS EVIDENCE BASED?

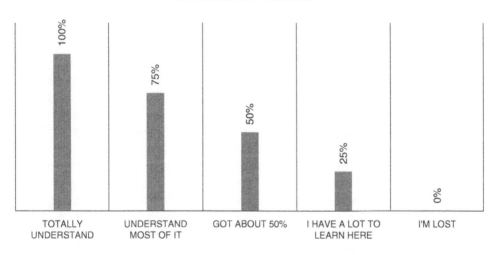

Figure 4.1 Self-reflection tool – how confident are you that what you do in school is evidence based?

DOI: 10.4324/9781003315728-5

Raising attainment

"The fourth-grade slump" is a term used to describe the phenomenon where the literacy attainment gap widens most significantly and there is a decrease in reading skills when children are between the ages of 8 and 11 (Chall et al., 2009). The slump occurs disproportionately more for those children living within areas of poverty (Chall et al., 2009). There have been various initiatives throughout the UK to rebalance the inequalities, including the City Challenge, The London Challenge, and in Scotland, the Attainment Challenge (Sosu & Ellis, 2014). This study took place in a Scottish Attainment Challenge Local Authority with such a task (Sosu & Ellis, 2014). They recognised that any new intervention being considered should be scrutinised, perhaps by including a pilot, before a program would be rolled out across the wider authority. There was recognition that reading comprehension was a skill which underpinned all learning because of the evidence that metacognitive, cognitive, and study skills have the potential to raise attainment across the curriculum (Ahmadi et al., 2013) and these can be taught (Haller et al., 1988).

All evidence-based materials are not of equal value. We may have seen on the TV adverts which make claims that 9 out of 10 women would use this beauty cream. Yet, if we were to drill down, we might find that the cream was compared with those that used no cream at all and those that did were under 25 and had not yet been introduced to wrinkles. This type of study may have an evidence base within it but of very different quality of evidence to those undertaken in random controlled trials where every attempt is made to remove conditions that could reduce the reliability or validity of the study (Torgerson, 2008; Torgerson & Torgerson, 2013). Therefore, before rolling out any new intervention, we need to ensure that the claims that it makes live up to the reality and will be successful within our context (Boyle et al., 2010; Moir, 2018).

Chapter 3 discusses several multiple strategy reading comprehension approaches which had been considered. This had highlighted the potential impact of the work undertaken by McCartney, Ellis, and Boyle of Strathclyde University in 2015. However, although their findings were promising, their study had no control condition to determine whether the intervention was more effective than the regular literacy curriculum in schools. Also, the key principles had been taken from two larger-scale studies (James-Burdumy et al., 2009; Shanahan et al., 2010) in America (see Chapter 3), yet they had not been tested or been applied in practice in Europe; therefore, Authority X wanted to undertake a study to ensure these approaches were robustly evidence based for their UK context. Given that the approach was to develop higher-order reading skills and that it had roots with Strathclyde University, it was named the Strathclyde Higher Order Reading (SHORS) project, which incorporates the ideas and strategies within this book.

The study aimed to find out whether, for elementary-school-aged pupils in mainstream environments, children undertaking the SHORS programme made improvements in:

- Reading comprehension.
- Decoding.

- Children's self-reported use of metacognitive and cognitive strategies.
- Children's self-reported reading habits.

compared to children undertaking regular literacy lessons during the same time frame. In addition, the study wanted to identify what were the facilitators/barriers to implementing the intervention?

After a preliminary investigation (Moir, 2017), it was found that 74 children (66 + 10% to allow for attrition) would be needed and, as such 35 males and 39 females aged between 9 and 10 were invited to take part from four local authority mainstream schools (Moir et al., 2020).

Measuring impact

Impact was measured using:

- The Wechsler Individual Achievement Test (Wechsler, 2005) – Second Edition (WIAT-II[UK]) reading comprehension scale to measure reading comprehension.
- Reading habits were measured by asking children at pre- and post-assessment periods: *How often do you read at home per week?*
- A readiness questionnaire to gauge the teacher's readiness to implement the approach (see Chapter 11).
- Teacher's semi-structured post-intervention interview where teachers were asked:
  o Do you feel that taking part in this project has altered how you approach teaching literacy?
  o If so, in what way?
  o Do you think students found the literacy instruction any different?
  o How do you know?
  o Can you identify any strengths of the approach?
  o What aspects were the challenges?
  o What would help overcome these challenges?
  o Do you feel being part of this project impacted your:
    - Knowledge of reading instruction?
    - Skill of delivery?
  o Was the coaching effective?
  o What could have made you feel more supported in applying this approach?

- Children's self-reported record of strategy use with questionnaires developed within the McCartney et al.'s study (2015) as seen in Figure 4.2.
- Fidelity Observation Schedule, which aims to measure the fidelity of implementation for the intervention group only (see Chapter 11 for discussion and details). It takes an event sampling approach, where a tally of events, such as types of instruction, was used to organise observational data for subsequent analysis as seen in Figure 4.3.

Reading: Pupil self-assessment   Name: ....   Class ....

	I do this often	I sometimes do this	I hardly ever do this
Prepare your mind – What's this text about? What do I already know? What's most likely to happen? Do I need to have an opinion and/or understand facts and events?			
Visualise – If this were a film, what would I see? What would this information look like as a diagram/flowchart?			
Hear a voice reading aloud in your head – can intonation help me make sense? Will accents help me track who's speaking?			
Rephrase – In my own words, that means...			
Summarise as you go along – What do I know so far? What don't I know yet? What do I need to know?			
Hold your thoughts as you read – Why am I being told this now? How does this information link together? What am I assuming that isn't in the text?			
Question – Does this seem likely? Does this "ring true"?			
If you don't understand it . . . Stop. Re-read.			
If you STILL don't understand . . . find the problem word. Does it remind me of other words or parts of words? Can I guess a bit from the context? Who can I ask? If none of these, **LOOK IT UP.**			
Link to wider experiences – How does this relate to what I already know/have read/ have done? What was new to me? Would I have reacted in the same way?			
Think about the crunch points – At what point(s) could this have gone a different way?			
Wonder to yourself – What could happen in a different context? Why might this person/group behave like this?			

Figure 4.2 Children's self-reported record of strategy use with questionnaires developed within McCartney et al.'s study (2015)

Fidelity Classroom Observation Form (Page 1 of 3)

Observer
School/Class
Teacher/TA
Date
Time in   Time out
No. of Pupils
Points to Note (disruptions, etc.)

Only to be used to measure fidelity of intervention teacher teaching the intervention group (not the control group).

Fidelity Classroom Observation Form (Page 2 of 3)

Teacher Prompts	Tally	Notes
Prepare your mind – What's this text about? What do I already know? What's most likely to happen? Do I need to have an opinion and/or understanding of fact and events?		
Visualise – If this were a film, what would I see? What would this information look like as a diagram/ flow chart?		
Hear a voice reading aloud in your head – Can intonation help me make sense? Will accents help me track who's speaking?		
Re-phrase – In my own words, that means ….		
Summarise as you go along – What do I know so far? What don't I know yet? What do I need to know?		
Hold your thoughts as you read – Why am I being told this now? How does information link together? What am I assuming that isn't in the text?		
Question – Does this seem likely? Does this "ring true"?		
If you still don't understand it . . .. Stop. Re-read.		
If you STILL don't understand …. Find the problem words. Does it remind me of other words or part of words? Can I guess a bit from the context? Who can I ask? If none of these, LOOK IT UP.		
Link to wider experiences – How does this relate to what I already know/ have read/have done? What was new to me? Would I have reacted in the same way?		
Think about the crunch points – At what point(s) could this have gone a different way?		
Wonder to yourself – What could happen in a different context? Why might this person/group behave like this?		
Was a graphic organiser used?	Yes	No

Fidelity Classroom Observation Form (Page 3 of 3)

Direct teaching of Vocabulary - Did the teacher

	Not Observed	Minimal/ Erratic	Partially Effective	Good	Excellent
Teach new words as they arise?	N/O	1	2	3	4
Fix it in their memory; aim to marinate them in the words -word was; talk tasks; lots of examples?	N/O	1	2	3	4
An example of what this is	N/O	1	2	3	4
An example of what this is not....	N/O	1	2	3	4
What has a similar meaning?	N/O	1	2	3	4
What has the opposite meaning?	N/O	1	2	3	4
Do I know any parts of the word (roots)? Chunk it into meaningful parts.	N/O	1	2	3	4
How many syllables?	N/O	1	2	3	4
What does it mean?	N/O	1	2	3	4
What sound does it begin with? Are there smaller words in it? Does it rhyme with anything?	N/O	1	2	3	4

Figure 4.3 Fidelity observation schedule

Design and procedure

The authority had been tasked with raising attainment across the curriculum (Sosu & Ellis, 2014); therefore, it was important to ensure that the children and teachers taking part in this study were not taking part in any other project that could reduce the reliability of this study (Torgerson, 2008; Torgerson & Torgerson, 2013). The pilot had showed that four schools were required to take part. All children within the authority had taken part in national reading comprehension tests using the New Group Reading Test (NGRT) four months prior to the intervention period. This facilitated initial analysis, a matching process, to ensure that reading levels in the participating intervention and control groups were at a similar level before introducing SHORS, as this would make later data analysis more reliable (Torgerson, 2008; Torgerson & Torgerson, 2013).

Participating schools were randomly allocated either to the control condition (which would continue with their regular literacy lessons) or the intervention condition (for which teachers would be taught and coached in the SHORS methodology and this approach would be used within their classrooms).

Five teachers (an opportunistic sample of those who taught the relevant year groups within the candidate schools) took part. Three were in the intervention condition and two were in the control condition.

Details of the intervention group

SHORS is a methodology that allows teachers to blend the approach with their teaching resources in whole-class and group settings (Moir et al., 2020). It recommends a flexible, embedded approach, which can be easier for teachers to implement than a more prescriptive approach (Moir, 2018).

As training is one of the most effective ways of improving teachers' practice (García et al., 2011; Joyce & Showers, 2002), teachers within the intervention condition were offered, and took part in, a two-hour training session which provided details of the SHORS approach. There were opportunities for discussion about the underpinning theory, reading comprehension instruction, and how to effectively embed the programme in the daily routine of the classroom. Information on reading comprehension strategies, videos of exemplar instruction, handouts, and classroom reminders, including a classroom poster, were provided for the teachers.

For eight weeks four, 45-minute sessions took place per week where teachers used the SHORS intervention programme to deliver the literacy lessons within children's regular school day. During this period, the researcher visited the classes and undertook fidelity observations using the form in Figure 4.2. There was also time for the researcher to offer coaching support, to offer opportunities to discuss the intervention, and to ensure that there had been no misinterpretations regarding the intervention (Joyce & Showers, 2002). Full details of the approach are outlined in Part 2; however, here is an overview. The intervention entailed the following text comprehension strategies and illustrative "key messages" being overtly taught, emphasised, and referred to throughout literacy classes, for example:

- Children would actively engage in reading comprehension by consciously accessing their prior knowledge: *"Prepare your mind. What is this about?"*
- Children would develop and answer questions about important ideas in the text: *"Wonder to yourself. Does this seem likely?"*
- Children would visualise what a text means: *"If this was a film, what would I see?"*
- Children would clarify points of misunderstanding: *"If I don't understand, stop, re-read. If I still don't understand, find the problem word. Does it remind me of other words? If necessary, look it up."*
- Children would make inferences around the text: *"How does this relate to what I already know? What was new?"*
- Children would summarise: *"What do I know so far? What do I need to know?"*
- Children would retell the main points of the text: *"In my own words, that means ..."*

In addition, the children were encouraged to use hand gestures when using a strategy, as this increased their metacognitive awareness (Courtney & Gleeson, 2010). After there had been an opportunity to read something as a class, there would be post-reading reflection time where the teacher encouraged high-quality discussion time. Children were asked questions to deepen their understanding, for example, how the story could have ended differently ("*crunch points*"). In addition, the teacher was encouraged to use McCartney et al.'s (2015) approaches to vocabulary development for unfamiliar words. Text organisational structures were also encouraged. Finally, the teachers were asked to take extra care to ensure the texts which were selected would be of interest.

Details of the control group

The control teachers and children did not receive any training, materials, or coaching but instead continued to follow their regular literacy practices. However, they were asked to schedule literacy lessons of equal time to the intervention classes (4 x 45 minutes per week during the 8 week intervention period).

Results

Reading comprehension

When improvement in reading comprehension for the SHORS group was compared with that of the control group [using the standardised measure WIAT-II (Wechsler, 2005)], the results showed a large effect size d = 0.81 (see Chapter 3). Analysis showed that the level of this effect size could only be attributed to the intervention and not measurement error. Figure 4.4 shows the improvements made by the SHORS intervention group compared with the control group undertaking their normal literacy lessons.

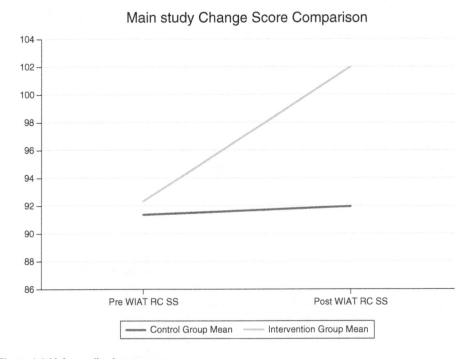

Figure 4.4 Main results change score

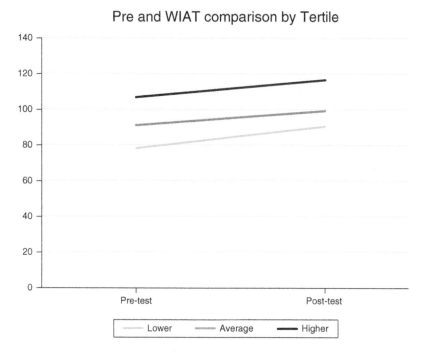

Figure 4.5 Results for ability sub-groups

In order to see whether this was an intervention that could be effectively used for all children or one which disproportionately supported children with different degrees of reading ability, further analysis was undertaken. Children within the intervention group were assigned to sub-groups according to their pre-intervention reading ability test scores (lower ability, average ability, and higher ability). As each sub-group's reading comprehension improved over the intervention period to the same degree (as seen in Figure 4.5), the intervention can be described as a universal approach, one equally effective for those of any ability (Moir et al., 2020).

Decoding target words

When improvement in decoding skills for the SHORS group was compared with that of the control group [using the WIAT-II (Wechsler, 2005)], the results showed a medium effect size of $d = 0.56$ for reading decoding skills. This indicates how related the different sub-component parts of reading skills interact. By increasing the skill in one area (comprehension) this had also increased skill in another area (decoding) (Moir et al., 2020).

Children's self-rated scales of strategies used

When improvement in children's self-report of strategy use was compared for those in the SHORS group to those in the control group (using Figure 4.1), the results showed children in the latter group's self-rating of their use of strategies had increased, with an effect size of $d = 0.75$. This shows that the SHORS intervention helped children become more aware of strategies to help their reading and they were more likely to use them (Moir et al., 2020).

Frequency of reading at home as reported by the children

Children in the intervention group reported reading more frequently at home during the intervention period than prior to the intervention period, with an effect size of $d = 0.88$. Interestingly, however, the control group reported reading less frequently during the intervention period than prior to the intervention period (Moir et al., 2020). So children within the SHORS group were more likely to read more at home, yet children in the regular literacy group had less motivation to read at home.

Readiness questionnaire

Before the intervention started, those teachers in the intervention condition were asked to complete a readiness questionnaire (Moir, 2019). We will discuss these in detail in Chapter 11. However, the reason for its use is to make sure that the teachers who are being asked to take on board a new initiative have the time, capacity, and motivation to do so. Within this study, all teachers in the intervention condition completed the readiness questionnaire, stating that they were willing and able to take part in the study. After the study, it was found that of the three intervention teachers, two taught within a school where the Head Teacher requested all staff to attend the training. Observations by the researchers suggested that they were exceptionally interested in the intervention and highly motivated to implement it as described (Moir et al., 2020). They started staff discussions regarding the approach and valued their and the Head Teacher's support when taking the approach forward.

Fidelity observations

The intervention teachers were observed during weeks 3 and 6 of the 8-week intervention period. They were scored in relation to how many of the essential components of the intervention were witnessed.

Although all three intervention teachers implemented the approach they did so to different degrees (Moir et al., 2020). As the intervention period went on, the evidence supporting its implementation increased, perhaps due to teachers' increase in confidence and skills as time passed (Moir, 2018). When the reading comprehension data was mapped against the teachers, it became clear that the more the teacher stayed true to the intervention, the greater the impact it had on children's comprehension skills. Figure 4.6 shows the more they implemented the ideas, the better the children's reading outcomes. For example, when the teacher was observed implementing 6 of the essential features or core components of SHORS the effect size was $d = 0.52$ but if the teacher was observed implementing 15 of the essential features of SHORS approach the effect size jumped to $d = 0.82$ (Moir et al., 2020).

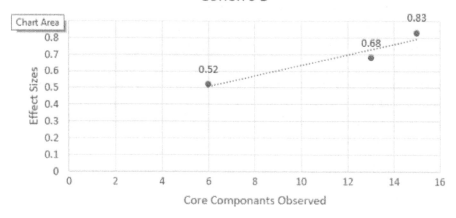

Figure 4.6 Correlations between teacher effect size and core components observed

Post-intervention teacher qualitative discussion

Conclusions were drawn that, although all three teachers implemented the intervention, they did so to different degrees (Moir et al. 2020). At the end of the intervention period, when asked if they had adhered to the criteria on the readiness questionnaire, two of the teachers said fully while one said she had found this too difficult within her context. The researcher could then categorise the intervention teachers into one of two distinct groups: teachers who implemented the programme to either a higher degree or a lesser degree (Moir et al., 2020). The two sub-categories continued to be evident when the teachers of the two groups reported different stances regarding the intervention during the post-intervention semi-structured interviews.

The feedback from the teachers who had implemented the intervention to a higher degree elicited quotes regarding SHORS, which were 100% positive. Quotes which illustrate this include:

> "The approach was different in that it was a methodology rather than something that was bought in, another resource".

> "It is more explicit in the use of strategies and I found myself asking questions that I wouldn't otherwise have asked".

> "It was very child friendly".

> "Children throughout the school were better at articulating what they imagined".

> "It enabled children to really get in a text where they had never had the opportunities to do that before".

"Also the strategies for vocabulary were very useful, far better than just putting the word in a sentence".

"All the teachers have taken this on board and all are very positive".

"They enjoyed hearing about the different strategies and children liked using the symbols which helped them to reinforce their understanding".

"When the children were working with classroom assistants that the children knew more about strategies than the Classroom Assistants and so X (one of the "intervention" teachers) did some training with them".

"It helped discussion skills; for even a short piece of text, children can understand it and talk about it with far greater depth".

"The discussion is far more pupil led".

"The strategies helped the children to really develop higher-order thinking instead of rushing through a task".

This school had implemented the intervention at a whole-school level and had gone on to train classroom assistants in the approach after it was noticed that the children doing SHORS knew more about strategies than the assistants (Moir et al., 2020).

The teacher who implemented SHORS, but to a lesser degree, was still positive about SHORS but felt much of the approach had already been evident in their practice prior to the training and coaching. Quotes which illustrate this include:

"I already knew what to do although it did put a new slant on things and perhaps made me more explicit when discussing strategies".

"I would always have talked about things like visualising but perhaps was not as direct in how I taught it".

"I used similar strategies so they probably were not that aware of anything different".

As stated, all three intervention teachers implemented the approach within their classrooms. However, those that took the approach more to heart, those that implemented it better, those with more enthusiasm and motivation to be involved in the project gained better results (Moir et al., 2020). Empowerment came up as a theme for all implementation teachers, yet the data showed that this was for very different reasons. The teachers that implemented the programme more fully felt that the children were empowered in their learning because now they had tools they could use autonomously when the learning got difficult (Moir et al., 2020). The teacher who implemented the programme to a slightly lesser degree said the children were empowered by having their views captured within real-life research. However, as seen in Figure 4.6, the important point is that the children of the teachers who stayed closest to the intervention programme had the biggest positive increase in their reading comprehension and associated skills (Moir et al., 2020).

Interpretations

The study showed that the intervention had a positive impact on children's reading. The effect sizes were such that it could be concluded that the change in scores could only be attributed to the effect of the intervention and not any kind of test measurement error (Moir et al., 2020).

There were several core elements to the intervention, one being the emphasis on direct teaching of strategies. This and the other core elements of the intervention will be the focus of Part 2. Direct teaching has an existing evidence base and its impact on learning outcomes cannot be underestimated (Wilson & Haugh, 2009). The teacher taking the time to directly teach strategies and model them for children is important (Moir et al., 2020). Yet, within a jam-packed curriculum, the level of reinforcement required to ensure children use strategies automatically can be overlooked. Classroom quality discussions can unlock the door to comprehension that children need to develop their understanding of topics and if a child does not understand, they will lose any motivation or drive for learning (Manning & Payne, 1993).

It is also important to note that all children within the intervention group's comprehension developed. These approaches are not only for the "high fliers" or for those who struggle or have additional support needs. This study found that all children benefitted from the instruction equally and therefore it can be regarded as a universal approach (Moir et al., 2020).

Those teachers within the intervention group said that they found it delightfully indulgent to take the time to have good quality classroom discussions. They recognised the value of using good questions and their ability to include everyone. They described how the learning seemed far deeper than before. As time went on, they felt their own skill in asking good questions increased. Similarly to research (Ketch, 2005), they felt these conversations were having unexpected bonuses of helping the teacher understand and relate to the class in a way that they had never done before. Indeed, it seemed like dedicating time to these discussions about learning was time well spent, for the depth of learning meant that as time passed, it was a far more time efficient approach overall (Moir et al., 2020). The feedback also indicates that the process made the teachers reflect on their own practice and notice their approach, feedback, and questioning techniques; indeed, they became more metacognitively aware (Moir et al., 2020).

Implementation science links

Teachers within the intervention group reported they enjoyed the experience, had learnt a lot, and thought that the ideas within the approach were easy to implement (Moir et al., 2020). What made the approach so easy to implement was the fact that it was a very flexible approach, where teachers took on board feedback from children to inform their next steps rather than having to rigidly conform to strict lesson plans (Fixsen et al., 2009). While the ideas had been based on reading research and were implemented within literacy lessons, the approach increased understanding and critical thinking across the curriculum. The same strategies could help develop meaning regardless of whether it was a literacy lesson, a mathematics lesson, or a geography lesson (Baker, 1994; Bensley, & Spero, 2014; Moir et al., 2020). The more that a teacher invested in the intervention, the more that they got out of it, the more enjoyable the experience had been and the more impact that they had (Moir, 2018). Although some resources were provided to the intervention teachers with posters and videos, the approach needed no large bank of expensive materials. Indeed, the most effective materials were those aid memoirs which the children created for themselves (Moir et al., 2020). These pupil-generated resources had the power to become far more meaningful for the individuals than glossy mass manufactured resources ever could be (Moir et al., 2020). Perhaps the reason this approach was so easy to implement was the fact that there was nothing incredibly different from what is generally recognised as good teaching pedagogy (Moir, 2018). Yet, the approach made elements of good teaching and learning more evident, but there was no mystic involved. The approach increased teacher confidence alongside their level of skill.

Pupil empowerment

What can be more empowering than knowing what to do when things have not gone to plan? The children within the study had been taught explicitly by their teacher what to do when they got stuck (Moir et al., 2020). They no longer needed to run to the teacher and ask for help. They became autonomous learners. They knew strategies they could employ and increased their confidence as a learner, improved their self-efficacy, their motivation to learn, and their levels of creativity (Davies et al., 2013). The by-product of this was more uninterrupted time for the teacher to engage in a targeted and meaningful way with their class (Moir et al., 2020).

Best practice teaching and learning

This study did not identify any new strategies. What it did was evidence how strategies should be taught. It also highlighted some particularly useful strategies and ideas and identified some key elements that when in place facilitate a positive learning environment. Talk of learning, discussions about ideas, and creativity around concepts was far more evident in the classroom than talk of assessment, scores, or outcomes (Driscoll & Pianta, 2010). The learning journey was flexible and responsive in a way that enabled even the most reluctant learner to become more involved in their learning process. Even those teachers of high skill level and years of experience enjoyed engaging in the approach, as they found it reassuring that what they had always assumed to be evidence based was indeed best practice (Moir et al., 2020).

Reading habits

We have already mentioned the "fourth-grade slump", a phenomenon which occurs in upper primary/elementary schools whereby reading comprehension skill decreases (Chall et al., 2009). This was evident in the study's control group, who reported reading at home for pleasure less as they got older. However, those children within the intervention group not only were resilient to the slump, but their amount of reading at home statistically significantly increased (Moir et al., 2020). Taking part in the study had had a positive impact on children's reading habits. As children read more, it is likely this additional practice led to an increase in reading skill (Davis, 2010). This then perpetuates a positive cycle, where reading more increases skill, which increases self-efficacy, which leads to more reading, and so on.

Conclusions

This study evaluated the approaches detailed within this book and confirmed them to be of high impact within the UK context, as was the case for US contexts. The strategies raised reading comprehension outcomes for all children. It reinforces previous works which suggest that explicit instruction in metacognitive strategies significantly benefits pupils' learning. In addition to this, both teachers and pupils enjoyed employing these methods and increased children's motivation to read more for pleasure while not in school (Moir et al., 2020).

Self-reflection tool

How confident are you that what you do in school is evidence based? Where would you position yourself in Figure 4.7? How different is this to how you assessed yourself in Figure 4.1?

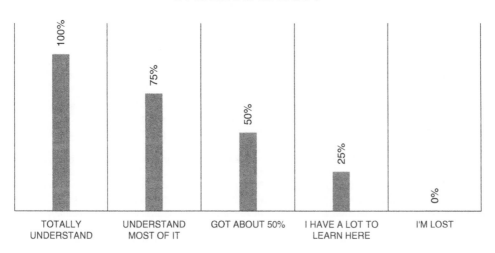

HOW CONFIDENT ARE YOU THAT WHAT YOU DO IN SCHOOL IS EVIDENCE BASED?

Figure 4.7 Self-reflection tool – how confident are you that what you do in school is evidence based?

Were you surprised by any of the study findings?

What checks do you make that what you are implementing in school is evidence based?

How could you ensure quality evidence?

How do you currently measure your impact?

Once you have thought about these questions, identify one or two areas that you want to enhance. How are you going to do this? What is the easiest way for you to measure your impact?

What am I going to try?	How can I measure impact?

Figure 4.8 Chapter planning tool

You can always come back to this chapter to build on other areas of practice; however, it is better to keep it simple and easy to manage changes by only committing to one or two at a time.

References

Ahmadi, M. R., Ismail, H. N., & Abdullah, M. K. K. (2013). The importance of metacognitive reading strategy awareness in reading comprehension. *English Language Teaching, 6*(10), 235.

Baker, L. (1994). Fostering metacognitive development. *Advances in Child Development and Behavior, 25*, 201-239.

Bensley, A., & Spero, R. (2014). Improving critical thinking skills and metacognitive monitoring through direct infusion. *Thinking Skills and Creativity, 12*, 55-68.

Boyle, J., McCartney, E., O'Hare, A., & Law, J. (2010). Intervention for mixed receptive – expressive language impairment: A review. *Developmental Medicine & Child Neurology, 52*(11), 994-999.

Chall, J. S., Jacobs, V. A., & Baldwin, L. E. (2009). *The reading crisis: Why poor children fall behind*. Harvard University Press.

Courtney, A., & Gleeson, M. (2010). *Building bridges of understanding: A whole school approach to children's comprehension development*. www.sess.ie/resources/

Davies, D., Jindal – Snape, D., Collier, C., Digby, R., Hay, P., & Howe, A. (2013). Creative learning environments in education – A systematic literature review. *Thinking Skills and Creativity, 8*, 80-91.

Davis, D. (2010). *A meta-analysis of comprehension strategy instruction for upper elementary and middle school students* [Unpublished PhD dissertation, Vanderbilt University].

Driscoll, K. C., & Pianta, R. C. (2010). Banking time in head start: Early efficacy of an intervention designed to promote supportive teacher-child relationships. *Early Education and Development, 21*(1), 38-64.

Fixsen, D., Blase, K., Naoom, S., & Wallace, F. (2009). Core implementation components. *Research on Social Work Practice, 19*(5), 531-540.

García, G., Pearson, D., Taylor, B., Bauer, E., & Stahl, K. (2011). Socio-Constructivist and political views on teachers' implementation of two types of reading comprehension approaches in low-income schools. *Theory into Practice, 50*(2), 149-156.

Haller, E., Child, D., & Walberg, H. (1988). Can comprehension be taught? A quantitative synthesis of "metacognitive" studies. *Educational Researcher, 17*(9), 5-8.

James-Burdumy, S., Mansfield, W., Deke, J., Carey, N., Lugo-Gil, J., Hershey, A., … Faddis, B. (2009). *Effectiveness of selected supplemental reading comprehension interventions: Impacts on a first cohort of fifth-grade students*. NCEE 2009-4032. National Center for Education Evaluation and Regional Assistance.

Joyce, B., & Showers, B. (2002). Student achievement through staff development. In B. Joyce & B. Showers (Eds.), *Designing training and peer coaching: Out needs for learning*. National College for School Leadership.

Ketch, A. (2005). Conversation: The comprehension connection. *The Reading Teacher, 59*(1), 8-13.

Manning, B. H., & Payne, B. D. (1993). A Vygotskian-based theory of teacher cognition: Toward the acquisition of mental reflection and self-regulation. *Teaching and Teacher Education, 9*(4), 361–371.

McCartney, E., Boyle, J., & Ellis, S. (2015). Developing a universal reading comprehension intervention for mainstream primary schools within areas of social deprivation for children with and without language-learning impairment: A Feasibility Study. *International Journal of Language & Communication Disorders, 50*(1), 129–135.

Moir, T. (2017). *Developing higher-order reading skills in mainstream primary schools: A metacognitive approach* [Doctoral dissertation, University of Strathclyde].

Moir, T. (2018). Why is implementation science important to intervention design and evaluation, within educational settings? In *Frontiers in education* (Vol. 3, p. 61). Frontiers.

Moir, T., Boyle, J., & Woolfson, L. M. (2020). Developing higher-order reading skills in mainstream primary schools: A metacognitive and self-regulatory approach. *British Educational Research Journal, 46*(2), 399–420.

Shanahan, T., Callison, K., Carriere, C., Duke, N., Pearson, D., Schatschneider, C., & Torgesen, J. (2010). *Improving reading comprehension in kindergarten through 3rd grade. IES practice guide what works clearinghouse.* NCEE 2010–4038. US Department of Education.

Sosu, E., & Ellis, S. (2014). *Closing the attainment gap in Scottish education.* www.jrf.org.uk/sites/default/files/jrf/migrated/files/education-attainment-scotland-full.pdf

Torgerson, D. J. (2008). *Designing randomised trials in health, education, and the social sciences.* Palgrave Macmillan.

Torgerson, C. J., & Torgerson, D. J. (2013). *Randomised trials in education: An introductory handbook.* Education Endowment Foundation.

Wechsler, D. (2005). *Wechsler individual attainment test – Second UK edition (WIAT-II UK).* Psychological Corporation.

Wilson, J., & Haugh, B. (2009). Collaborative modelling and talk in the classroom. *Language Education, 9*(4), 265–281.

PART 2
Practice and pedagogy

5 Metacognition and mindset

This chapter is concerned with metacognition and how this links with mindset (Dweck, 2008). If you are an educator, in order to help your own metacognitive thinking, ask yourself what is it that made you want to become an educator? What are the most rewarding aspects of the job? What did you think would be the most rewarding aspects? Has your mind changed? Reflect on the impact you have had, and can have, as a teacher or educator today. You will no doubt have plenty to draw from.

Metacognition: what is it?

Within education, from time to time, different words become fashionable, the new answer to all our problems. Metacognition now seems in vogue. This previously terrifying word is now used in everyday practice. The role of metacognition in development, and its use in academic skills, is widely recognised both in research and practice. But what is your understanding of it?

How well do you understand metacognition and mindset? Where would you position yourself in Figure 5.1?

What does metacognition really mean? I remember hearing about metacognition myself and it got neatly tied up into the regularly used phrase: "thinking about thinking". At its best, this phrase neatly sums up complex ideas, but perhaps, it does not do the concept justice. So, let us unpick the metacognition together.

Metacognition is a process which is employed when we consider and are aware of our own cognitive capabilities. It is a highly complex process, one which when you unpick increasingly grows arms and legs. For we are not talking about one process, but many interacting processes (Education Endowment Foundation, 2020). This is recognised by the prefix "meta" inferring the multiplicity. The complexity has led to a variety of different terms used and little consistency in how they are used or their exact definitions. This has led many to, understandably, shy away from the word or overgeneralise its meaning, with potentially over-simplistic definitions like "thinking about thinking". No wonder it is hard to know exactly what to do when asked to teach "metacognitively".

DOI: 10.4324/9781003315728-7

HOW WELL DO YOU UNDERSTAND METACOGNITION AND MINDSET?

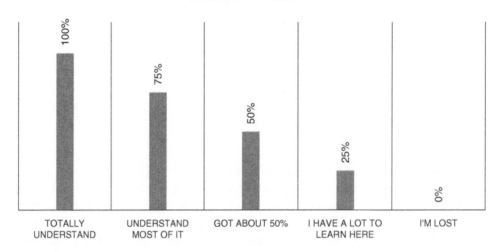

Figure 5.1 Self-reflective tool – what is your current understanding of metacognition and mindset?

Metacognition a working definition

The concept of metacognition was first outlined in 1971 by Flavell, who defined it as our knowledge of our own cognitive processes. This early definition concerned itself fully with the knowledge components which could be subdivided into three parts (Flavell, 1971; Garner, 1987; Myers & Paris, 1978):

- Knowledge of self. This type of declarative knowledge of "ourselves as learners" is relatively stable across time. We know if we like certain formats or materials and we have an idea about how successful we are at these various different types of thinking skills, for example, a preference for verbalising answers over writing them or a preference for multiple-choice questions or a belief that we are good/bad at problem-solving skills. This type of knowledge of self has also been referred to as intra-individual differences (Garner, 1987; Paris & Oka, 1986; Paris et al., 1984). Incidentally, declarative knowledge is knowledge that can be expressed in a declarative sentence or an indicative proposition. "Knowing-that" can be contrasted with "knowing-how" (also known as "procedural knowledge"), which is knowing how to perform some task, including knowing how to perform it skillfully (Flavell, 1971; Garner, 1987; Paris et al., 1984). We can think about our thinking here by, for example, asking ourselves how we normally solve problems. Some students may think and process information best in a quiet library, while others may focus better surrounded by their favourite music. Sometimes it depends on how well we understand the task (Flavell, 1971; Garner, 1987). For example, when I am learning something new I like quiet but as I become more familiar with the material, I like background music on. With greater awareness of how we gain knowledge, we learn to regulate our behaviour to optimise learning. We begin to see how our strengths and weaknesses affect how we perform. The more conscious of ourselves we are as learners, the more we can use this knowledge to our advantage as autonomous and efficient learners.

- Knowledge of tasks we face. This type of knowledge also falls under the category of stable declarative knowledge, yet this time the knowledge of "ourselves as learners" includes information regarding the population's abilities in certain tasks, for example, we know it is easier to read a book when you have knowledge of all the associated vocabulary within the topic being read (Cain & Oakhill, 2014; McCartney et al., 2015). This has also been referred to as inter-individual differences which compare the child's abilities in one area with the child's abilities in other areas (Paris & Jacobs, 1984). One child may find it easier to learn physics than French, while another finds the exact opposite. We can think about our thinking here by, for example, reflecting on the task. Here we can ask ourselves about our task preferences and yet again, the greater the knowledge we have about ourselves, the more we can use this knowledge to our advantage (Flavell, 1971; Garner, 1987; Paris et al., 1984).
- Knowledge of strategies. This is a more procedural type of knowledge being information on commonly accessible strategies, for example, typically taught strategies like mnemonics, repetition, or chunking (Flavell, 1971; Garner, 1987; Paris et al., 1984). We know that all these approaches work for most people and therefore have been referred to as "universals". We can think about our thinking, for example, by asking ourselves what universal strategies we know that could be employed to help finish the task. What strategies have you used before?

Different theorists have built on Flavell's ideas, so that now it is generally recognised that besides metacognitive knowledge, a second component of metacognition is metacognitive experiences (Myers & Paris, 1978; Paris et al., 1984). Metacognitive experiences focus more on self-regulatory aspects. For example, a student reading a geography question may not understand a word within a question. If the learner recognises this, they may employ some sort of self-regulatory activity to try to help them finish the task. Activities that may help the learner are things like using a dictionary or looking at a glossary. This action requires the learner to recognise when they have not understood something and then do something about it to get back on track. For this action to occur, the learner needs to be reflective and have the ability to think critically.

Figure 5.2 takes the concept of metacognition described here and illustrates the connections between different components.

This model tries to simplify what is a complex process. This is a model that could easily be criticised for being overly simplistic. However, it shows some of the principal components and serves to highlight that just because a learner may understand a strategy, they may not have engaged in the learning process sufficiently to want to use it. If they do not fully understand the question, have they understood the task? Do they have any goals they want to achieve when beginning the task? It takes a conscious effort to stop and employ a fix-up strategy and unless you are motivated to do so, it is unlikely to happen (García-Rodicio & Sánchez, 2014). If you get distracted when you are reading, it can be difficult to re-engage (Rellinger et al., 1995). Sometime a loss of focus is enough for a learner to realise that they are not in the learning zone to continue and decide to stop the task and do something else.

Metacognitive skills become increasingly important as we grow and are expected to learn more independently (Education Endowment Foundation, 2020). A classroom assistant may be available to keep a child on task by acting as their external metacognition. Yet if the classroom assistant is always there to prompt and re-engage, the child will never develop the skill to work independently. We as educators cannot continually support a child

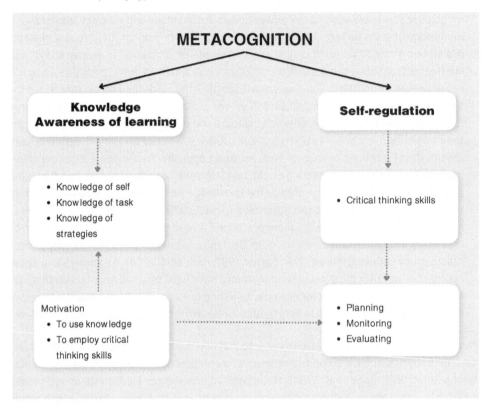

Figure 5.2 A model of metacognition by the author

to stay on task in the classroom and expect them to know how to stay on task when working independently at home. Teachers can be exceptionally good at spontaneously offering feedback, but how are we ever going to develop autonomous learners without having a strategy around how to take this high level of scaffolding away? Our face-to-face time with our children, therefore, needs time dedicated to teaching strategy and process: how to regulate attention, how to think critically, how to question, and how to monitor myself as a learner. These skills can and should be nurtured in young children. For example, the ability for 3-4-year-old children to self-reflect leads to more reflective and therefore better behavior and outcomes (Lavery, 2008). However, these metacognitive skills become even more important as children become adults partly because learning in colleges/universities depends on autonomous learning, for there is no longer a classroom assistant on the side lines (Liu & Stapleton, 2014). Ultimately, functioning as an adult in the world of work requires these metacognitive and reflective skills. Not only does metacognition support reading, but also our self-concept, our social cognitions, and our actions (Ruddell & Unrau, 2004).

The metacognitive cycle

Learners who have good metacognitive awareness know what they are good at, and the mere fact that we know we are good at something makes us more likely to be motivated to continue doing it (Moir, 2019). We therefore have more opportunities to practice the skill and continue to get better at it. Knowing that we are good at something includes not only the knowledge about our ability (knowledge of ourselves as a learner) to do the task but also all the information we hold regarding how we feel about doing the task, how we might be able to do the task effectively (knowledge of strategies) and details around the intricacies of the task (knowledge of the task).

As we undertake the task, certain aspects may become easier as our knowledge of strategies increases or the depth of information around an aspect of the task increases. We are then continuously updating our understanding of ourselves as learners and what areas we are good at and the areas that we could improve on. The adaptation of our perceptions in relation to the task is called our metacognitive regulation. We need to begin by reflecting on the task. What do we know about it? Then creating some sort of plan of action based on this knowledge of what works and what does not. Then, as we begin to undertake the task, we are continually monitoring our progress. Are we on the right track to achieve our goal? As we progress through different stages of the task, we update our metacognitive knowledge (of yourself, strategies, and tasks), as well as updating our knowledge of the subject and skills. The cycle continues: plan, monitor, evaluate while we continually adjust our metacognitive knowledge of self, strategies, and task. Experienced learners go through these stages automatically. However, developing learners benefit from support and explicit instruction to work through this process (Moir, 2019).

Let us consider an example with reference to the metacognitive cycle in Figure 5.3. Harry has been given this task:

"Answer this riddle: What has a neck but no head?"

Harry starts with some knowledge of the *task* (he has done some riddles before) and of *strategies* (he remembers riddles often rely on words with double meanings; he also knows he should look for any clues). His knowledge of the task (riddles try to trick you – when we think of a "neck" we often think of a person. Could there be an inanimate object that has a neck? Harry plans to brainstorm objects that could have a neck. He then evaluates some of his options; a bottle or a shirt? He then *evaluates* his overall success by putting the neck of a shirt or bottle into a sentence to check that the word could be used that way. If it makes little sense, he may adjust his plan and try another strategy and once more update his metacognitive knowledge. We all go through this type of process, although often we are unaware of it (EEF, 2020). Learners with lots of different cognitive and metacognitive strategies could be described as more effective learners as they have will have more ways to get "unstuck" and thereby have more motivation to persevere with a task (Chan, 1994; Moir, 2019). However, it is better to know and use a few strategies well than many strategies superficially. Although we can intuitively learn and use strategies, the research continues to affirm that we all benefit from being taught them clearly and explicitly (Haller et al., 1988).

Mindset

Carol Dweck[1] did a huge amount of mindset research and she identified two basic "mindsets". We will not have the same mindset about everything; however, we tend to either be someone with a fixed mindset or growth mindset (Dweck, 2008). A person with a fixed mindset tends to believe that abilities and attributes are permanent. A person is good or evil. A person's

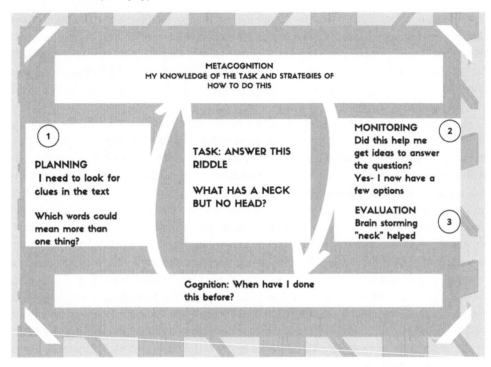

Figure 5.3 The metacognitive cycle

abilities are intrinsic and therefore you will either be good or bad at languages, science, or art. They believe that there is little a person can do to overcome their limitations and there is no point in investing time and energy into something that you cannot do well straight away. The person with the growth mindset believes that people and their abilities are open to change. Dweck has studied the phenomenon across the world and the impact of mindset in different contexts, for example, schools, parenting, and workplaces. She asserts that the way we think (fixed or growth) can have a tremendous impact on our actions and, therefore, on our outcomes. A person with a growth mindset is likely to believe they can get better at something (Dweck, 2008). They have a sense of self-efficacy and, therefore, are more likely to give things a go (Bandura, 1976). They perhaps do not expect to be good at something straight away, yet they will invest time and keep trying. Alternatively, those with a fixed mindset may try something once but will be more likely to give up quickly if they do not immediately show an aptitude for the task (Dweck, 2008). As they do not believe they can get better at the task, they have a low sense of self-efficacy and therefore will be unlikely to try. They believe that they will only show themselves to be a failure and will be far more fearful about taking risks. They believe you are naturally talented or not. As they believe their aptitude is intrinsic, there is less likelihood that they will study (Dweck, 2008). Having a fixed mindset can close you off from many learning opportunities, as there is no recognition that investing time and effort into practice is valuable. They are likely to become demotivated quickly. Dweck's research showed that when a student with a fixed mindset failed, they are likely to blame factors out of their control, for example, the weather was not right, the exam paper was stupid. However, a person with a growth mindset is likely to be more metacognitively aware. They are likely to consider their knowledge of the task and the strategies they used to plan how to improve their ability in the future. They will take time and invest energy into the task and continue to monitor and evaluate their progress as their learning develops (Dweck, 2008).

If we want to develop children's metacognitive skills, there are certain things that we can do to instill a growth mindset which positively impacts on learning. Attribution involves teaching students to attribute the quality of their work to factors over which they have control, such as effort, study time, and the use of appropriate strategies; and not to attribute the quality of their work to fixed attributes over which they have no control, such as talent, ability, prior learning, or intelligence (Law, 2009). This will develop the learners' self-efficacy – their belief that they can develop their learning skills (Bandura, 1976; Law, 2009).

How does mindset develop?

A baby's desire to explore, their curiosity without fear, irrespective of danger, suggests we come into the world having a growth mindset. Babies do not give up when trying to roll over, or stand up, or walk for the first time. They make many attempts and are never downhearted or thwarted by their inability to master a skill the first time. So when could a fixed mindset occur? Dweck's work shows that some children from as young as four years old can have become fearful of failure as personified by the fixed mindset. Therefore, there is something in the atmosphere, the environment, that influences this change and as we know, the biggest influence of a young child is the surrounding people, predominantly Mum and Dad. The words we use with children are value laden and ultimately communicate to the child what is valuable or important in life. How can it be that saying a child is "clever" could be a bad thing? Surely this will support the child's self -esteem? However, saying a child is clever at something without reference to effort gives them the message that this new skill is intrinsic/fixed/genetically determined and out of the child's control. If my "cleverness" is innate and I have no control over this, then why should I work hard for something? It also communicates to the child that we value "cleverness" and, as children enjoy praise, they will want to continue to demonstrate "cleverness". There is little chance this child will do something that they are not good at in case it dispels the belief of "cleverness". We have no control over our "cleverness" but it will influence what we decide to do or not do. As the child learns about the world from those around them, the praise that we give to children powerfully influences their mindsets (Dweck, 2008).

When praising children, we should instead concentrate our attention on the effort that a child makes. Effort is something the child can be in control of (something never possible with levels of "cleverness"). So, saying "I can see you tried really hard there" or "well done, that took some perseverance", the child receives the message that the thing of value is effort and we can all decide how much effort we put into something in the future. The important part is the process which the child is in control of, not the finished product or outcome. Praise will not produce success, but it can instill a confidence in learners to try to give things a shot even when they are learning a new skill.

How to help children's mindset grow?

- First, we need to notice our own mindset. What words are we using to describe our own mindset? I can be guilty of saying "I can't", especially when particularly stressed; "I can't parallel park."
- It is worth thinking about how your parents and teachers praised you. Did this instill a fixed or growth mindset? Do you say things like "he's bad"? Do you think children are open to change? How do you think you can change?
- Mind your language. What do you say when you make a mistake? Do you berate yourself? Do you get annoyed and say things like "I'm so stupid". Do you avoid doing things when you think you might make a mistake? Or are you the type of person who invests time and energy into getting better at things?
- There are some things that we will have a growth mindset on while others we can be quite fixed about. While we all have different dispositions and aptitudes for things, we should be mindful whether this is cutting off our options and opportunities.
- Children are sponges, taking their cues about the world from the surrounding adults. While reading through some of the previous points, what conclusions have you drawn about your mindset? Whatever it is, children are quick to pick up on it. It will probably be on a very subliminal level that they will recognise what is of value: effort or cleverness. Give feedback that links to progress, effort, determination, resilience, and grit.
- Talk about the learning progress, not the outcomes. Help children to celebrate the learning journey. See the value in drafting and redrafting to facilitate development, growth, and improvement. Get them to set their own goals and decide on how they will fulfil them. Throw out the laminator, which only prizes a finished and perfect end product. Pursuit of perpetual perfectionism is unachievable, and aiming for this can instill some serious mental health issues.
- If we believe people can grow, develop, and change with determination and practice, we must also be mindful that the language we use does not describe people in terms of fixed attributes. Saying "you're stupid" or "you're naughty" only serves to reinforce these negative attributes and reduce motivation to become anything or anyone positive. As mentioned previously, even describing people in terms of positive fixed attributes like "you're smart" makes people stressed that one day the secret will get out and they are really stupid. Praise for positive fixed attributes is potentially a forerunner to imposter syndrome.

In my spare time, I dance Argentine Tango, a fabulous hobby which I have engaged in for many years. People often will say to me "I can't dance" or "I have two left feet". My gut reaction is often to ask whether they have had any lessons to which the reply is often "no". My question then has to be, "if you have done no dance lessons, why should you be able to dance?" I have spent increasing sums of money on private and group lessons and spent over five to ten hours a week practicing dancing for years. I think the world would be unfair if someone who had not invested so much in learning Argentine Tango was just as proficient as me with no practice or effort. There are some skills that we can be predisposed towards being good at, but to get really good at anything requires dedication, time, and commitment.

Often we are unaware of the language that we use which can reinforce a fixed mindset. Children are wonderful at picking up on this. The atmosphere that we create within the classroom will determine how safe children feel about being creative or confident to put their hand up when their answer may not be correct. It might be worth reflecting on what your school or classroom culture is like by considering:

- **Messages from symbols**. Actions, decisions, and situations are visible to people – and to which they attribute meaning. What do you have on your walls? Messages of triumph (laminated finished products) or messages of effort (drafts and redrafts of a project).
- **Messages from systems**. How your organisation rewards, measures, manages, and communicates what is important. Do you praise those children who get full marks or those who showed greatest improvement, made the best mistakes, or asked the best questions?

Research shows it is also worth teaching students how their brains are wired for growth. The beliefs that learners adopt about learning and their own brains will affect their performance. Research shows that when students develop a growth mindset as opposed to a fixed mindset, they are more likely to engage in reflective thinking about how they learn and grow. Teaching children about the science of metacognition can be an empowering tool, helping them to understand how they can literally grow their own brains.

Self-reflection tool

At the beginning of this chapter, you were asked to take a note of anything that you think might be useful to consider in the future. To help embed these ideas, take some time to answer the following questions and identify one or two things that you will do differently because of reading this chapter. It may be useful to do this in conversation with a peer or small group of staff together.

How well do you understand metacognition and mindset? Where would you position yourself in Figure 5.4? How different is this to how you assessed yourself in Figure 5.1?

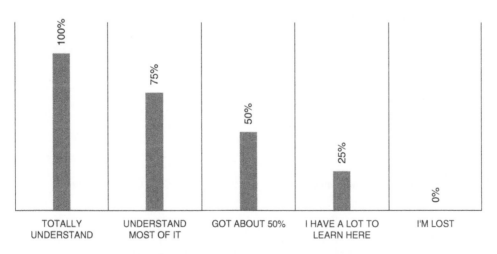

Figure 5.4 Self-reflection tool – how well do you now understand metacognition and mindset?

What is it that made you want to become a teacher?

What are the most rewarding aspects?

What do you currently know about metacognition?

How do you/could you convey to your pupils that you have high expectations of them?

How do you/could you convey to pupils that understanding the concept is more important than correct answers?

How do you/could you show that it is all right to make mistakes?

How do you/could you create a collaborative rather than a competitive environment?

How do you/could you convey to pupils the benefit of the lesson?

How do you/could you enable all children to see themselves as successful learners?

How do you/could you offer different learning or reading choices?

How do you/could you encourage collaboration with peers?

How do you/could you model a growth mindset?

What do the symbols and displays on your walls tell you about what you value?

What do your reward systems tell you about what you value?

Once you have thought about these questions, identify one or two areas that you want to enhance. How are you going to do this? What is the easiest way for you to measure your impact?

What am I going to try?	How can I measure impact?

Figure 5.5 Chapter planning tool

You can always come back to this chapter to build on other areas of practice. However, it is better to keep it simple and easy to manage changes by only committing to one or two at a time.

Note

1   Additional details can be found in Dweck, C. S. (2008). *Mindset: The new psychology of success*. Random House Digital, Inc.

References

Bandura, A. (1976). Self-reinforcement: Theoretical and methodological considerations. *Behaviorism*, *4*(2), 135–155.

Cain, K., & Oakhill, J. (2014). Reading Comprehension and vocabulary: Is vocabulary more important for some aspects of comprehension. *L'annee psychologique (Topics in Cognitive Psychology)*, *144*, 647–662.

Chan, L. (1994). Relationship of motivation, strategic learning and reading-achievement in grade5, grade 7 and grade 9. *Journal of Experimental Education*, *62*(4), 319–339.

Dweck, C. S. (2008). *Mindset: The new psychology of success*. Random House Digital, Inc.

Education Endowment Foundation (2020). https://educationendowmentfoundation.org.uk/public/files/Publications/Metacognition/EEF_Metacognition_and_self-regulated_learning.pdf

Flavell, J. H. (1971). First discussant's comments: What is memory development the development of? *Human Development*, *14*(4), 272–278.

García-Rodicio, H., & Sánchez, E. (2014). Does the detection of misunderstanding lead to its revision? *Metacognition and Learning*, *9*(3), 265–286.

Garner, R. (1987). *Metacognition and reading comprehension*. Ablex.

Haller, E., Child, D., & Walberg, H. (1988). Can comprehension be taught? A quantitative synthesis of "metacognitive" studies. *Educational Researcher*, *17*(9), 5–8.

Lavery, L. (2008). *Self-regulated learning for academic success: An evaluation of instructional techniques* [Doctoral dissertation, ResearchSpace@].

Law, Y.-K. (2009). The role of attribution beliefs, motivation and strategy use in Chinese fifth-graders' reading comprehension. *Educational Research*, *51*(1), 77–95.

Liu, F., & Stapleton, P. (2014). Counter-argumentation and the cultivation of critical thinking in argumentative writing: investigating washback from a high-stakes test. *System*, *45*, 117–128.

McCartney, E., Boyle, J., & Ellis, S. (2015). Developing a universal reading comprehension intervention for mainstream primary schools within areas of social deprivation for children with and without language-learning impairment: A feasibility study. *International Journal of Language & Communication Disorders*, *50*(1), 129–135.

Moir, T. (2019). The psychology within models of reading comprehension and the educational psychologist's role in taking theory into practice. *Educational and Child Psychology*, *36*(3), 52–64.

Myers, M., & Paris, S. (1978). Children's metacognitive knowledge about reading. *Journal of Educational Psychology*, *70*(5), 680–690.

Paris, S. G., Cross, D. R., & Lipson, M. Y. (1984). Informed Strategies for Learning: A program to improve children's reading awareness and comprehension. *Journal of Educational Psychology*, *76*(6), 1239–1252.

Paris, S., & Jacobs, J. (1984). The benefits of informed instruction for children's reading awareness and comprehension skills. *Child Development*, *55*(6), 2083–2093.

Paris, S. G., & Oka, E. R. (1986). Children's reading strategies, metacognition, and motivation. *Developmental Review*, *6*(1), 25–56.

Rellinger, E., Borkowski, J. G., Turner, L. A., & Hale, C. A. (1995). Perceived task difficulty and intelligence: Determinants of strategy use and recall. *Intelligence*, *20*(2), 125–143.

Ruddell, R., & Unrau, N. (2004). Sociocognitive model of reading. In R. Ruddell & N. Unrau (Eds.), *Theoretical models and processes of reading* (pp. 1462–1523). International Reading Association.

6 Metacognition and motivation

This chapter is concerned with metacognition and how this links with motivation. As you read through, it might be useful to relate this reading with some frameworks discussed in Chapter 2 and reflect on how the messages assimilate. Here we will consider how we get into the right environment to learn. Think about what motivates you to learn? When are you "your best" learner?

Before we begin, what is your understanding of metacognition and motivation? Where would you position yourself in Figure 6.1?

HOW MUCH I UNDERSTAND ABOUT METACOGNITION AND MOTIVATION?

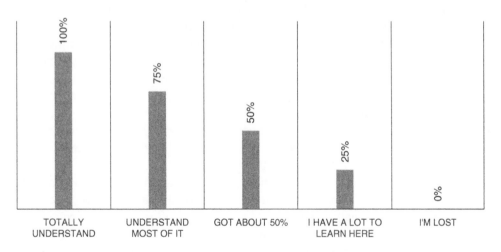

Figure 6.1 Self-assessment tool – how much do you currently understand about metacognition and motivation?

Nurturing motivation

Empirical studies have traditionally either focused on metacognition or motivation rather than fully appreciating the inseparable links between the two concepts (Law, 2009; Paris &

DOI: 10.4324/9781003315728-8

Oka, 1986). As metacognition, by definition, takes a conscious effort, there needs to be a desire or motivation to employ it (Chan, 1994). Metacognition requires being active and present in the learning process, a learning process we care about and are invested in. So, if we want our children to become good metacognitive learners, we need to get them to the place where they care about the task (Chan, 1994). If learners are to learn, they need to decide that they want to learn. Teachers cannot learn for them.

If motivation is linked so directly with metacognition, the next question becomes, how do we increase our children's motivation? Children need to want to be in our learning environment and we need to ensure that the learning environment feels safe. Most adults can reflect on times when they have been in a position when they should read or learn something, but we are so consumed with a worry or a stress that we just cannot concentrate. The same is true, if not more true, of children. The more safe and comfortable they feel, the more learning will take place. We will learn best if we all work within a "blame-free" classroom, either virtual or traditional. For Harry Potter lovers, there is a reason his poorest subject was potions. His relationship with Professor Snape was far from cordial. Children and young people need to know that:

- The teacher cares for them (Davies et al., 2013; Ruddell & Unrau, 2004; Sosu & Ellis, 2014). It is now recognised that one of the most important facilitators in learning is a positive teacher/pupil relationship. The connection between attainment, within-school connectedness, and positive, developing and restoring relationships are recognised as being at the core of effective schools. A focus on relationships and implementation of ideas like "connectedness" and "attunement" rather than authoritarian behaviour management approaches will enable more children to thrive. Think back to your own school experience. What was your best subject? How did you get on with your teacher?
- The teacher has high expectations of them (Moir, 2019; Sosu & Ellis, 2014). Extrinsic motivation is usually built through having high expectations, clarity, and fairness. A child will thrive when they realise your high expectations. It shows you think a great deal of them. Just be mindful that with these high expectations, you are giving the appropriate level of support: just enough support to get them there.
- If the teacher is bored with a lesson or a book, learners will recognise this and take part with similarly low energy levels. Yet, if the teacher appears motivated in the topic, their pupils will also be swept into enthusiastic engagement.
- Writing is often perceived as a punishment. It certainly was in the days of writing lines. Children may also see reading as a punishment. Try to understand what conclusions children have come to regarding tasks they are reluctant to do, what are the negative connotations they hold. Perhaps reframe the language you use, for example, making a sign rather than writing or telling a story rather than reading, to get more engagement. Having stimulating discussion prior to a writing activity allows children to fully explore their imagination and therefore gives them something they are interested in to write about. Alternatively, discuss with them exceptions: when have they enjoyed writing/reading? Listen to what they tell you and use the information to guide the activity. This will help change the fixed mindset "I dislike reading/writing" into one with more growth.
- High expectations differ from unfair expectations. Learning a new concept does not happen straight away; learning takes time. Sometimes there can be unfair expectations: "I told you X before", "you are in primary 6, so you should know this". Learning is a process,

and this will become clear as we continue through the chapters. Therefore, we cannot expect children to understand new concepts wholly and completely without time and practice. We cannot expect children to thrive if they have not had sufficient quality learning experiences. It is always worth checking what learning experiences a child has had. For example, a child who was in hospital for 6 months during their second year at primary school is likely to have missed many lessons on different phonics sounds. Later in school, the child is labelled as having poor literacy skills when these are skills the child has never been taught explicitly. It is not a problem with the child's learning ability, it has been a problem with the child's learning opportunity, yet the child could easily be labeled dyslexic. However, if these sounds are later taught, the child will catch up and there is no need for any intrinsic tags. Also, if two teachers have a job share and teach the same class, it is essential that adequate time is ring-fenced to ensure professional discussion to ensure that there are no curricular gaps. Unfortunately, when a child has not learned something, we attribute this to the child's inability, but could the consistency or quality of the teaching experience have been improved?

- It is more important to understand the question or task than to get the answer correct. In exams, this is recognised by the fact that a large share of the marks in many questions are gained by showing workings. We can all make silly arithmetical errors, but that is not important, as long as you understand the concepts. As the concept becomes more familiar, we should obviously then expect children to get the final answers correct, but initially, knowing HOW to tackle the problem is far more important.

- Mistakes are part of the learning process as they show us how to progress (Autin & Croizet, 2012). If a child is always getting full marks, the work is too easy and there is no challenge and ultimately no learning. Children will disengage from boredom. With every task, there should be opportunities for the learner to see what they can do better on next time.

- We all make mistakes, but not everybody learns from mistakes. It takes a metacognitive learner to look at the mistake and learn from it how to improve. Too often, we expect children to automatically reflect on their mistakes and learn from them. However, learning from mistakes is a reflective process. This is a skill that may or may not have been developed yet.

- It is possible to have procedural knowledge of a mathematics problem, for example, subtraction, and be able to work through a process yet not have a conceptual understanding of the purpose and function of subtraction in the real world. In order to fully engage children with problem solving, work through these problems in context first before moving onto abstract computations. This will make the task more meaningful and worthwhile.

- When we do not understand something, there is an opportunity to learn something. If a classroom has a very competitive edge, children will not feel secure enough to say that they do not understand. I remember being part of a class with this type of culture and the emphasis was on how many pages of the book you had "read" rather than the enjoyment or experience of reading. As you can imagine, with such a competitive environment I could leaf through dozens of pages, but had I understood it? No. Had it been a good learning experience? No. Did I enjoy reading? Certainly not then or there. An optimum environment is one that encourages collaborative learning, curiosity, and sees learning as a process while recognising the value of mistakes and taking time for learning.

- Create an atmosphere where everyone recognises everyone will get stuck at some point (Autin & Croizet, 2012). Have a class discussion about what you can do when you get stuck, for example, reread the question.
- It is good to help each other. Children learn as much being the helper as the child being helped. There can often be a reluctance by teachers to pair children of different abilities together, yet that is not taking advantage of the tremendous opportunities that mixed ability pairing yields. Not only is the child being helped learning (while adults can get on with other teaching duties) but the helping child is reinforcing their own learning. Incidentally, Van Ryzin and Roseth (2019) found peer learning has the added advantage of encouraging the development of empathic, collaborative, and a positive culture which reduced incidences of bullying within your classroom. Where possible, give students opportunities to learn by collaborating with peers. This not only improves their learning, but develops skills in collaboration and team building that are needed within the 21st century job market. Working individually in silence rarely relates to modern day occupations. Encouraging children to interview each other in schools can lead to more honest answers than if the teacher was asking the questions and also leads to a more participatory and empowering environment.

Teachers sometimes ask elementary questions, which, if answered incorrectly, can be humiliating. However, if the question is challenging, it is not humiliating to make a mistake. We all make mistakes when we learn. Indeed, that can be a huge part of how we learn. Encourage creative answers in your classroom, and do not be afraid to make mistakes yourself, as it will only make you more human and more relatable. A child who has been ridiculed for their mistakes, even in a joking way (many children do not understand the subtleties of sarcasm), will be less likely to engage in their future learning. Can you remember yourself or a friend being ridiculed when you were a child at school? How did it affect you/them?

Motivation: the right task

Before anything else, we need to be sure that our learners are in the right place to learn. As we have said, the links between motivation and learning are very strong, especially when considering metacognitive tasks (Chan, 1994). Often when our understanding breaks down, children can fail to employ "fix-up" strategies automatically, even if they know how to do so (García-Rodicio & Sánchez, 2014). Therefore, tasks and texts should be carefully selected to be of high interest in promoting maximum motivational engagement (Dörnyei, 2001). We can do this by:

- Articulating why the lesson is relevant to the real world so that they can understand its benefits and applications. Tell them why they should they learn it (Moir, 2019). How would this be beneficial? What is the use of this learning in real life? How could it be applied? It is also important to highlight that sometimes, the purpose might just be to read for pleasure and that, in itself, is of value. If this is articulated, you are giving children permission to immerse themselves in fiction. The OECD found that whether or not a child enjoys reading has a bigger impact on their outcomes than their socioeconomic status. Often reading is associated only with books, yet reading blogs and magazines can be equally valuable and potentially more so if they are a better fit for the learner's interests. If you know the child, you can use knowledge of their interests to tailor the reason for the lesson, for example, if a child is reluctant to write, but wants to develop friendships, reframe the purpose of that writing to be about developing the skills needed for writing cards and letters to friends.

- Create opportunities for students to see themselves as successful as motivation is linked to self-efficacy (Bandura, 1976). There is nothing more demoralising than when a task just seems far too complex (Findley & Cooper, 1983; Law, 2009; Paris & Oka, 1986). Pitching a task so that it is a challenge without being demoralising is difficult. Ensure that the challenge is moderate, but not excessively stretching. Too easy is boring, too difficult is demoralising; it is the Goldilocks principle of getting things just pitched at the right level of challenge (Rellinger et al., 1995). It can only be done effectively by getting to know the learner both directly and by having discussions with others who have also taught or teach the child. Transitions between schools is an obvious time to share information, yet the quality of transition information varies just as the level of engagement with transition information varies. How could your transition discussions be improved? Usually, transition information about children is more meaningful in face-to-face discussions rather than in the volume of paperwork. It is worth also considering that secondary school systems do not easily lend themselves to discussions between individual subject teachers to learn from each other who also teach a class or child. How could a secondary school system become more of an enabler of this type of discussion?
- Give students learning or reading choices where possible to increase their sense of autonomy (Schiefele et al., 1992). As adults, we are more likely to read a book that either we have chosen ourselves or has been chosen for us than one that is randomly handed out. Why would children be any different? Giving a child a book with a smile and telling them you think this story would interest them boosts the teacher/pupil relationship and encourages the child to read the book.
- Build a culture of reading where reading is visible and books are displayed and enjoyed (Moir, 2019). Some research shows that in high schools children are not encouraged to read for pleasure and it could be regarded as "something we don't need to do anymore" and there is less guidance given around what books children might enjoy.
- Give learners text organisational structures, like story maps (these will be discussed at length later in Part 2) and encourage them to be referred to within discussions.
- Always check that learners understand the basic vocabulary within the task/text/topic (McCartney et al., 2015; Cain & Oakhill, 2014). Direct instruction of vocabulary relates to the development of metacognitive strategies and has the potential to optimise comprehension skills. In other words, having the basic vocabulary for a topic is the basic building block for understanding. If you know the core vocabulary within a topic, the learning process will be much easier. If words within the text cannot be understood, inference and bridging strategies (higher-order strategies) would be useless (Cain & Oakhill, 2014). The table in Figure 6.2 can be used to do a vocabulary audit prior to starting a new topic so that the teacher can see what vocabulary needs to be explicitly taught. This should be regarded as a formative assessment tool to help the teacher, and definitely

not an assessment of the child. **It is very important that the children know that this information is to help you, the teacher.** I am sure you would feel anxious if you were given what could look like a test on a subject you have no prior knowledge of so the vocabulary audit needs to be carefully pitched.

Pupils give fairly accurate information on a vocabulary audit (McCartney et al., 2015). **Perhaps this could be something they could take home to discuss the words at the start of a unit. . .**

Key Unit Vocabulary	I know this word, it means.....	I have heard of this word, but I'm not quite sure what it means	I don't know this word

Figure 6.2 Vocabulary audit

- Once you have gathered the information from the vocabulary audit, explicit vocabulary instruction is necessary to ensure that the literacy gap between higher and lower achieving pupils is minimal. However, Rathvon's (2008) and Burns et al. (2017) research indicates that this is not regularly part of lessons. Intentional instruction in vocabulary is especially beneficial for children living in areas of high deprivation with a higher proportion of struggling readers. Furthermore, the "fourth-grade slump" has been partly attributed to the fact that too little direct instruction of vocabulary is taught to the upper primary school population. Also, from a culturally equitable perspective, prerequisite knowledge should never be presumed and topic-specific vocabulary needs to be taught to enhance understanding and inference skills. It is likely that even within a class of children from similar sub-cultural backgrounds, many children may not have had experiences that could have been taken for granted in mass-produced reading materials. In addition, when teaching children of varying socioeconomic backgrounds, there is potential for unintentional discrimination within the group (Moir, 2019). New ideas are not equally accessible to all children, regardless of their decoding skills. We can do this by taking a multisensory approach. Instead of only giving a definition for a word children are trying to learn, give them more things to attach meaning to the new word. Talk about what the word looks like or sounds like. The more "hooks" a child has for different words,

Figure 6.3 Multisensory vocabulary learning template

the more likely they are to understand them. Children learn new vocabulary better if the learning is active and social, for example, in drama skits or drawing maps with a partner. Also, they are more likely to learn new words if they quickly use the new word in their own writing. You could try a discussion around the multisensory vocabulary learning template in Figure 6.3.

Self-reflection tool

At the beginning of this chapter, you were asked to take a note of anything that you noticed related to the frameworks discussed in Chapter 2. Noticing these links will hopefully offer confidence in the application of the suggestions. To help embed these ideas, take some time to answer the following questions and identify one or two things that you will do differently because of reading this chapter. It may be useful to do this in conversation with a peer or small group of staff together.

But what is your understanding of metacognition and motivation? Where would you position yourself in Figure 6.4? How different is this to how you assessed yourself in Figure 6.1?

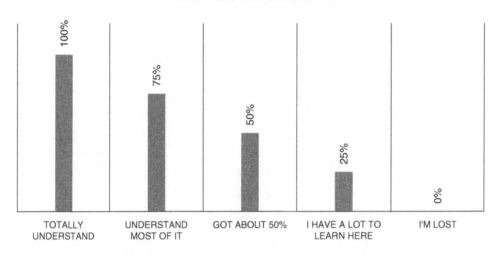

Figure 6.4 Self-assessment tool – ow much do you currently understand about metacognition and motivation?

What are the most rewarding aspects of teaching?

What do you currently know about motivation and metacognition?

What motivates you to learn?

How would you describe your classroom culture?

How do you know?

What would the children in your class say?

How do you/could you develop a good rapport with your pupils?

How do you find out about your pupils?

How do you/could you convey to your pupils that you have high expectations of them?

How do you/could you enable all children to see themselves as successful learners?

How do you/could you offer different learning choices?

How do you/could you encourage collaboration with peers?

How do you/could you use formative assessment information to ensure the challenge is moderately, not excessively, stretching?

How do you/could you better support vocabulary development?

Once you have thought about these questions, identify one or two areas that you want to enhance. How are you going to do this? What is the easiest way for you to measure your impact?

What am I going to try?	How can I measure impact?

Figure 6.5 Chapter planning tool

You can always come back to this chapter to build on other areas of practice; however, it is better to keep it simple and easy to manage changes by only committing to one or two at a time.

References

Autin, F., & Croizet, J. C. (2012). Improving working memory efficiency by reframing metacognitive interpretation of task difficulty. *Journal of Experimental Psychology, 141*(4), 610–618.

Bandura, A. (1976). Self-reinforcement: Theoretical and methodological considerations. *Behaviorism, 4*(2), 135–155.

Burns, M. K., Riley-Tillman, T. C., & Rathvon, N. (2017). *Effective school interventions: Evidence-based strategies for improving student outcomes.* Guilford Publications.

Cain, K., & Oakhill, J. (2014). Reading Comprehension and vocabulary: Is vocabulary more important for some aspects of comprehension. *L'annee psychologique (Topics in Cognitive Psychology), 144,* 647–662.

Chan, L. (1994). Relationship of motivation, strategic learning and reading-achievement in grade5, grade 7 and grade 9. *Journal of Experimental Education, 62*(4), 319–339.

Davies, D., Jindal - Snape, D., Collier, C., Digby, R., Hay, P., & Howe, A. (2013). Creative learning environments in education - A systematic literature review. *Thinking Skills and Creativity, 8,* 80–91.

Dörnyei, Z. (2001). *Teaching and researching motivation.* Longman.

Findley, M., & Cooper, H. M. (1983). The relation between locus of control and achievement. *Journal of Personality and Social Psychology, 44*(2), 419–427.

García-Rodicio, H., & Sánchez, E. (2014). Does the detection of misunderstanding lead to its revision? *Metacognition and Learning, 9*(3), 265–286.

Law, Y.-K. (2009). The role of attribution beliefs, motivation and strategy use in Chinese fifth-graders' reading comprehension. *Educational Research, 51*(1), 77–95.

McCartney, E., Boyle, J., & Ellis, S. (2015). Developing a universal reading comprehension intervention for mainstream primary schools within areas of social deprivation for children with and without language-learning impairment: A feasibility study. *International Journal of Language & Communication Disorders, 50*(1), 129–135.

Moir, T. (2019). The psychology within models of reading comprehension and the educational psychologist's role in taking theory into practice. *Educational and Child Psychology, 36*(3), 52–64.

Paris, S. G., & Oka, E. R. (1986). Children's reading strategies, metacognition, and motivation. *Developmental Review, 6*(1), 25–56.

Rathvon, N. (2008). *Effective school interventions: Evidence-based strategies for improving student outcomes.* Guilford Press.

Rellinger, E., Borkowski, J. G., Turner, L. A., & Hale, C. A. (1995). Perceived task difficulty and intelligence: Determinants of strategy use and recall. *Intelligence, 20*(2), 125–143.

Ruddell, R., & Unrau, N. (2004). Sociocognitive model of reading. In R. Ruddell & N. Unrau (Eds.), *Theoretical models and processes of reading* (pp. 1462–1523). International Reading Association.

Schiefele, U., Krapp, A., & Winteler, A. (1992). Interest as a predictor of academic achievement: A meta-analysis of research. In K. A. Renninger, S. Hidi, A. Krapp, & A. Renninger (Eds.), *The role of interest in learning and development* (pp. 183–212). Psychology Press.

Sosu, E., & Ellis, S. (2014). *Closing the attainment Gap in Scottish education*. www.jrf.org.uk/sites/default/files/jrf/migrated/files/education-attainment-scotland-full.pdf

Van Ryzin, M. J., & Roseth, C. J. (2019). Effects of cooperative learning on peer relations, empathy, and bullying in middle school. *Aggressive Behavior, 45*(6), 643–651.

7 How should I teach a strategy?

In this chapter, we will start by defining what a strategy is before we look at the process involved in teaching them. After all, it is the pedagogy, the "how", that makes the difference. It is hoped that talking about the "how" first will help you plan how you are going to implement appropriate strategies as you identify them from the following chapters in Part 2.

How confident are you in knowing what a strategy is and how you can teach one? Where would you position yourself in Figure 7.1?

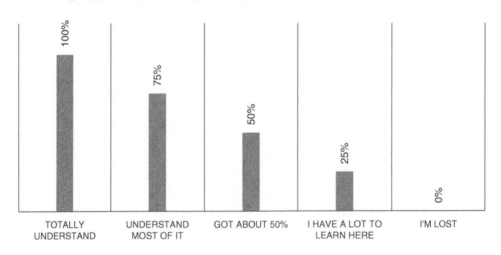

HOW CONFIDENT ARE YOU IN KNOWING WHAT A STRATEGY IS AND HOW YOU CAN TEACH ONE?

Figure 7.1 Self-reflection tool – how confident are you in knowing what a strategy is and how you can teach one?

What is the difference between cognitive and metacognitive strategies?

Strategies are discussed at length in Chapter 3, yet it is useful to remember that "strategies" are not the same as the skills typically outlined in curricular programs or teaching activities.

DOI: 10.4324/9781003315728-9

Shanahan et al. offered great insight into strategies in their work in 2010. They stated that a "strategy is not instructional activities such as completing worksheets. Worksheets rarely include instruction in what students should do actively in their heads to improve learning. A strategy is also not exercises that are aimed at giving students practice with skills such as sequencing or drawing conclusions, but that lack explicit instruction in how to think in these ways during reading". Instead, a strategy can be defined as a controlled conscious mental action that can be done during learning and that improves understanding. It takes motivation, effort, and awareness and, therefore, will never be done automatically.

There has been a great deal of debate that tried to unpick what makes a strategy a cognitive strategy rather than a metacognitive strategy. However, rather than categorising the strategies, it perhaps makes more sense to consider how we use the strategy. For instance, we may have a cognitive understanding of, say, "summarising" but we would have to employ this strategy in a deliberate and controlled way before we could call it a metacognitive strategy. It is the way we use the strategy – automatically or controlled – that perhaps determines whether it is a cognitive or a metacognitive strategy (Ahmadi & Gilakjani, 2012). This is perhaps why metacognition has been reduced to the definition "thinking about thinking" as it conveys the self-reflective stance needed to become metacognitive. Cognitive activities can be supported by learning tools, but here there is less concern about how these tools are used to control comprehension. When we are thinking metacognitively, we are concerned with meeting our personal goals; we reflect and evaluate. When we cannot work something out, when something fails to make sense, we have to notice that it is not making sense and then, with sufficient motivation, we will employ strategies to regain our understanding.

The case for explicit instruction of metacognitive strategies and study skills

In 2006, Eme, Puustinen, and Coutelet were some of the first researchers to recognise the importance of explicitly and directly teaching strategies. At this point, studies had shown that there was a general absence of explicit strategy instruction in schools and this was even less evident for metacognitive strategies than for cognitive strategies. Although some children will still be able to learn and employ strategies without this direct instruction, all children benefit from it (Adams & Carnine, 2003). Indeed, Sosu and Ellis argued in 2014 that teaching children about strategies with sufficient modelling and coaching can be one of the most effective things teachers can do to mitigate against the poverty-related attainment gap. Children in more affluent homes often benefit from more implicit learning through discussions and experience and it is hypothesised that other children can "catch up" if they receive quality explicit instruction (Pearson & Gallagher, 1983). By highlighting a strategy and explicitly teaching it, you are giving children a gift (Moir et al., 2020). You may be aware that some humanitarian appeals ask for donations which can give those who are hungry food. Other appeals ask for donations which are used to create wells or sow seeds. While both types are helpful, the former type encourages a dependency on others, while the second type encourages independence and autonomy. Similar can be said in teaching. We can either give children the answers to difficult questions or we can give them a bank of tools to work out the answers for themselves. Direct instruction of a strategy and then offering modelling and coaching support to build the child's skill in using the approach independently encourages them to be an active participant in their learning while fostering self-regulation skills, creativity, autonomy and maturity.

How to teach a strategy

There are various models of the stages involved in the teaching of strategies. Duke and Pearson (2009) described a four-stage process of direct teaching, modelling/think aloud, guided practice and application. However, these have become increasingly more detailed with the Education Endowment Foundation (EEF, 2020), outlining a seven-stage process, these being activating prior knowledge, explicit strategy instruction, modelling of a learning strategy, guided practice, independent practice, and structured reflection. These models all show a gradual transfer of responsibility for the application of the skill from the teacher (who initially has 95% – 100% responsibility before their proportion reduces steadily towards 0% responsibility) to the learner (who initially has 0% responsibility but their proportion grows towards 95% – 100% responsibility; see Figure 7.2).

This transfer of responsibility occurs gradually and at the learner's pace (Block & Pressley, 2007). Some children will require more scaffolding than others (Swanson & Hoskyn, 1998). However, as a general rule, all learners will need more reinforcement and coaching than teachers usually expect (Moir et al., 2020). Hopkins research suggests that if you want to make someone hear you, you will need to tell them at least seven times. We need reinforcement. Ultimately, when the teacher has created sufficient learning experiences, the pupil will have sufficient knowledge, confidence, and skill to employ the strategy without your support (National Literacy Trust, 2021). If you, as a teacher, give your students this gift where there is a real change in the brain during learning, the rest of their learning journey will be much smoother and easier for everyone.

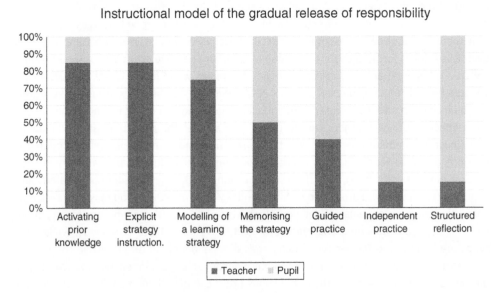

Figure 7.2 The process involved in learning a new strategy

There are three ways that the brain can change when learning. This first way is a chemical change in the neurons and occurs when learning is in our short-term memory. After one brief exposure to new learning this is where the information is likely to be stored by your learners. However, we are unlikely to remember anything and are likely to forget the new information unless there are opportunities to reinforce this learning. The second way our brain can change in learning is a structural change where the information from short-term memory is transferred to long-term memory. This takes time, yet this is when the learner will start to independently use, remember, or apply the learning. Only after many years of practice would the third type of brain change occur. This is when large sections of the brain repurpose themselves to accommodate what it realises is very important information in a process known as neuroplasticity. An example of this is where experienced taxi drivers' brains show large sections dedicated to route planning.

While generally speaking, we do not need our brains to change as significantly as the latter type, we need a sufficient quality learning experience to ensure that the strategy becomes embedded within long-term memory. If there is any doubt, over-model. Make it what you do. It is in the later stages that children become more independent.

As children are learning a strategy, they cannot problem solve with complex data. Start with the simple use of the strategy and contexts which are more familiar, while the basics of a strategy is still being understood. Only when the strategy is more fully embedded is the learner to tackle the manipulation of complex data. Let us go through each of the steps a teacher can go through to explicitly teach a strategy.

Step 1: Activate your prior knowledge

We all have good days and less good days. Sometimes our minds are so busy that we find it hard to engage in anything. Pushing forward with a task without acknowledging this can waste time and be a frustrating experience. The mere fact that we attune to our bodies and think about whether we are focused on what we are doing is great for realigning ourselves. Noticing that we are motivated will increase our motivation. Alternatively, if we realise we do not want to do the task, we may talk ourselves into it. "I'll do this for 15 minutes and then I will allow myself to do something else." Or "I don't really want to do this but the benefits of engaging in it will be X, Y, and Z". Consciously recognising our learning disposition enables us to get into the learning zone.

Whenever we are starting a new task or new learning, getting the class together to initially think about what they already know will help prime and support additional learning. The discussion helps all individuals to delve into their long-term memory and remember anything related. If we are learning a new strategy, we may begin by asking what we already know about strategies. Which strategies are particularly useful? When should I use strategies? Revisiting this existing knowledge will provide a solid foundation for the new learning. We may identify certain pieces of vocabulary that perhaps we should cover before moving on. The more we can remember, the more the learner will have to draw on, and it will be easier to internalise new concepts. The teacher is the facilitator of the discussion. The teacher is prompting the class, encouraging them to talk and share ideas. The better the quality of discussion, the more memories, thoughts, and ideas will be activated.

Step 2: Explicit strategy instruction

Within this stage, the teacher will lead a discussion about the new strategy that they are introducing. They will name the strategy and discuss why it might be a useful strategy and when it could be used.

Step 3: Modelling of a learning strategy

Within this stage, the teacher is showing or modelling to the students how to apply the strategy. The teacher may have a book that they read aloud. The teacher will stop throughout the reading the say to the class what they are thinking. The technique "think aloud" is very useful here and is where the teacher verbalises to the class what they are thinking to ensure that the process is as transparent as possible (Bereiter & Bird, 1985). In so doing, this overt approach of the use of a controlled mental process is revealed so that learners can gradually use it automatically. The teacher will recount to the class what thoughts, feelings, expectations, or questions the text raises for them. It will be necessary to repeat this process several times for any new strategy that is being introduced. The transfer of the skill is gradual and modelling a "think aloud" process once will be inadequate in equipping children to systematically use the approach themselves. It is recommended that the "think aloud" process be demonstrated at least six times for each strategy before this type of scaffolding is withdrawn.

Once the learners are familiar with the use of "think alouds", they could be asked to model to the teacher what they are thinking as they read, thereby providing a valuable formative assessment that can shape future instruction. A well-prepared teacher will be familiar with the text they are planning to read to the class, will have identified whether it lends itself to the strategy that they are teaching, will have planned when they are going to stop for demonstration of the "think aloud" process, and will have some ideas to develop a discussion about the strategy's usefulness.

Step 4: Memorising the strategy

Here, the teacher is doing what they can to support the transmission of the new strategy from short-term memory to long-term memory. They may provide some visual tools as reminders. These can be in the form of anchor charts (see Figure 7.5 below) and lists of strategies. These visual tools have the greatest impact when the children have designed and created them for themselves. The teacher will facilitate discussion to see whether the learners are really grasping how to use the strategy and the benefits of doing so. It is also helpful to discuss when this strategy might be more or less useful than other strategies that they have previously learned. Continue to encourage children to be conscious of the narrative of their thinking by hearing a voice "reading aloud" in their heads. In order to make the use of the strategy even more evident, ascribe a hand gesture to the strategy and boost strategy awareness by doing the hand gesture in tandem with the strategy use (Baker et al., 2014; Courtney & Gleeson, 2010; Parrish, 2010; Raphael & Au, 2005). Children are more empowered to learn when the learning is personalised to them and therefore it is better to get the pupils to decide what the hand gesture should be. Take photographs of the children doing the hand gesture and display them. All humans have a memory bias for material that can be processed

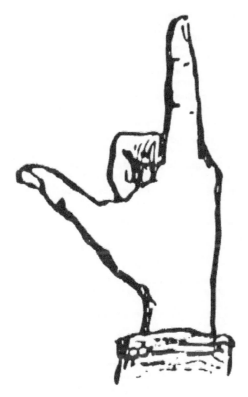

Figure 7.3 A hand gesture for where there is a link or connection identified

with a reference to the self. For example, putting a word in a sentence regarding the individual increases spelling accuracy by 20%.

Figure 7.3 is an example of one of the hand gestures used in the study outlined in Chapter 4. Its use was encouraged when children tried to link what was being read to something that happened in their own experiences. The hand gesture was trying to emulate an "L" to remind children they were "Linking."

The more that the learners can be involved in creating the memory aids, the better. Have the visuals in prominent places.

Figure 7.4 shows an example of a poster used in the study in Chapter 4 to remind a child of known strategies for reading. We will look at these strategies in more detail in Chapter 8.

Anchor charts can also help. These are clear detailed accounts of a strategy and how to use it written in age-appropriate language. These are best if co-created with the children to give them ownership and increased awareness of the strategy. Having them visible in the room can also help retention. Figure 7.5 for an example of an anchor chart for the strategy called visualising.

Anything that a teacher and a pupil can do to make the use of a new strategy as explicit and visible as possible should be encouraged. Children will better remember the things that they have created or drawn.

Prepare your mind- What's this text about? What do I already know? What does the author want me to think? Do I need to have an opinion, understand facts and events or just let myself believe?

Visualise- If this were a film, what would I see? What would this information look like as a diagram / flowchart?

Hear a voice reading aloud in your head- Can intonation help me make sense? Will accents help me track who's speaking?

Re-phrase- In my own words| that means...

Summarize as you go- What do I know so far? What don't I know yet? What do I need to know?

Hold your thoughts as you read- Why am I being told this now? How does this information link together? What am I assuming that isn't in the text?

Question- Does this seem likely? Does this 'ring true'? Do I understand all of this?

If you don't understand: Stop. Re-read.

If you STILL don't understand- find the problem word. Does it remind me of other words or parts of words? Can I guess a bit from the context? Who can I ask? If not, LOOK IT UP

Link to wider experiences- How does this relate to what I already know? What I have read? What I have done? What was new to me? Would I react in the same way?

Think about the 'crunch' points- At what point(s) could this have gone a different way?

Wonder to yourself- What could happen in a different context? Why might this person / group behave like this?

Figure 7.4 Strategy reminder poster similar to those used in Moir's 2017 study

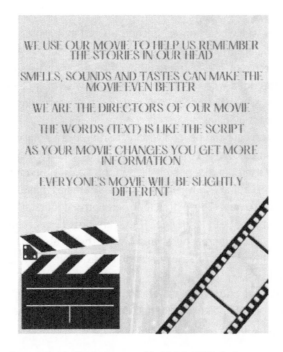

Figure 7.5 Anchor chart example similar to one used in Moir's 2017 study

Step 5: Guided practice

Within a crammed curriculum, the temptation could be to move on to a different strategy too quickly. However, without giving the learners sufficient time to practise, the use of the strategy could undo some of the hard work done. Guiding children as they practise using the strategy will build confidence and also help them decide for themselves when it is the best time to use what strategy. There is still a role for the teacher, assisting and guiding where necessary. It is like learning to ride a bike. Initially, the learner needs a lot of support, but eventually they will be able to stay fairly steady. However, unless this period is followed with opportunities to ride a bike, it is unlikely the learner will have sufficient skill and confidence to be considered a bike rider. Also, many car drivers believe it is only after having passed your driving test that you really learn the skill. It is the practice of driving that makes you develop the skill of driving – not getting your license.

Engaging with the learners and encouraging quality discussion enables depth of understanding and increases their ability to use the strategy co-dependently before independently. Allow time for peer discussions (Davies et al., 2013). When children are asked to take part in quality discussion, teachers often believe that they can go off topic. Therefore, do not expect all children to know how to have productive discussions. This is another skill that may need to be taught. To avoid this, provide clear guidance on what should be discussed and model how this guidance can be used.

Step 6: Independent practice

Here, the teacher has created an autonomous learner. All the scaffolding support has enabled them to know what strategies should be used when and how. They have a knowledge of themselves as learners and are conscious of the task and the process of learning. Again, the learner needs the opportunity to use the strategy independently.

Step 7: Structured reflection

Unfortunately, few students will stop and reflect on their learning unless encouraged to do so. Questions or quizzes could encourage children to think about how and when they have used strategies and what ones may be more successful in the future for different tasks. This develops the individual's knowledge of themselves as learners and promotes their more general metacognitive skills (Moir et al., 2020).

The transfer

Although this is considered step 7, the reflective skills are essentially what makes a strategy a metacognitive strategy and therefore the whole 7 step process requires reflective thought throughout.

We are ultimately working towards the learner's independent use of a strategy. If you feel as though you have gone through all of these steps sufficiently and the child is still not independently using the strategies, you will need to revisit the modelling and coaching steps and try to make the approach even more explicit. Children's learning varies and some children will require a great deal more modelling and practice time than others. With this in mind, it is better to teach one or two strategies really well rather than many superficially. When you are moving on to the teaching of a new strategy, always revisit the ones previously learned from time to time, practice them and ensure that they are still accessible for use by the children. In order to prevent cognitive overload, it is best to use familiar topics and simple syntactic structures when teaching a new strategy and move on to less familiar topics or more complex texts when the strategy you are focusing on is more embedded. This will support transference of the skill (Moir et al., 2020).

Once a task or problem is completed, encourage their reflective skills by asking questions like:

- How did we figure this one out?
- Which of the strategies worked and why?
- How (else) could we have figured it out?
- If you didn't solve the problem, which strategy would have worked and why?
- If you did solve it, which other strategy would have helped?
- Where else have we seen this strategy work well?
- Under what conditions is this strategy useful? For example, spectacles are always useful, but particularly if you have read the question carefully and drawn a diagram.

These questions can be referred to as a form of "bridging" and are key to the development of thinking skills (Haywood, 1988).

Before moving on to the next chapter to look more closely at different strategies, it might be worth doing an audit of your current strengths in this area and use it to see how you want to develop your skills (see Figure 7.6). It might be worth doing an audit frequently to remember the important steps involved in teaching a new strategy.

1: Activating Prior Knowledge	Rating: 1 - rarely 5 - almost always				
	1	2	3	4	5
I ask children to think "What's this strategy?"					
I ask children to think about "What do I already know?"					
I ask children to think about "Do I have an opinion?"					
I ask children to consider whether they are focused on this task (perhaps on an interest scale 0 - distracted to 5 - very interested.					
I ask children to think about how they feel about the task.					
I check in with students.					
I talk about my own prior knowledge in this area.					

2: Explicit strategy Instruction	Rating: 1 - rarely 5 - almost always				
	1	2	3	4	5
I explain to students what the strategy is.					
I explain why the strategy helps with the task.					
I offer opportunities for discussion about when to apply the strategy.					
I give examples of when the strategy can be used.					
I check that they really understand.					

3: Modelling of a Learning Strategy	Rating: 1 - rarely 5 - almost always				
	1	2	3	4	5
Prior to a lesson I identify the strategy I want to model. What is it and why might it be useful?					
I prepare a lesson by thinking about where I stop and how I will explicitly explain my thinking.					
I recognise that a one-off modelled lesson of a strategy is insufficient in systematically using the strategy.					
I talk with students about the value of using strategies to understand what they read so that they understand that strategies are important to both the assignment at hand and to life in general.					
I do "think alouds" which are oral verbalisations of underlying cognitive processes.					
I read a text, stopping occasionally to explain what I am thinking and how I am approaching the text/problem.					
I model my thinking by stopping at different stages of the task and explaining my thinking/conclusions/questions.					
Students are asked to think aloud during reading as a kind of formative assessment to guide instruction.					
I discuss the strategy towards the end of the lesson.					
I use a think aloud to illustrate a strategy on (at least) six occasions.					

4: Memorising the Strategy	Rating: 1 - rarely 5 - almost always				
	1	2	3	4	5
I check if pupils have understood the strategy.					
I check if pupils can remember the key aspects of the strategy and its main purpose, through questions and discussion.					
I keep strategies visual and visible.					
I remind students to use not only the strategy they just learned but also others they already know.					
I offer tips on when to use the strategies.					
I encourage children to hear a voice "reading aloud" in their heads.					
Where appropriate, I encourage memory through the use of hand gestures. I get the children to decide what hand gesture they will use when they use a strategy.					
I ask my students to create a list of their strategies they know.					
I ask my students to have the list of strategies nearby when they are working.					
I ask my students to produce a poster with all the strategies they know and use.					
I ask my students to create anchor charts. These are clear detailed accounts of a strategy and how to use it written in age- appropriate language. It is best if co-created with the children to give them ownership and increased awareness of the strategy.					

5: Guided Practice	Rating: 1 - rarely 5 - almost always				
	1	2	3	4	5
I structure the discussion to complement the text/task, the instructional purpose, and the learners' ability and grade level.					
I develop discussion questions that require students to think deeply about text.					
I ask follow-up questions to encourage and facilitate discussion.					

I have students lead structured small-group discussions.					
I guide and assist students as they learn how and when to apply the strategy.					
I guide students through focused, high-quality discussion.					
I help students practice the strategy until they can apply it independently.					
I encourage them to keep their visuals close by and refer to them.					
Our discussions among students or between the students and myself go beyond simply asking and answering surface-level questions to a more thoughtful exploration of the text. Through this type of exploration, students learn how to argue for or against points raised in the discussion, resolve ambiguities in the text, and draw conclusions or inferences about the text.					
I encourage collaboration, not competition.					
I read aloud and ask students periodically about what's happening, what the story is about, or what they think is going to happen.					
I facilitate a discussion by using a variety of higher-level questions that prompt the students to interpret the text.					
Adapting for younger students, I read a selection aloud, and have students discuss it with a partner and then report back to the class. To start a discussion at that point, I can ask students questions such as whether they think the character did the right thing.					

6: Independent Practice	Rating: 1 – rarely 5 – almost always				
	1	2	3	4	5
I understand independent practice can play an important role in developing self-regulation and metacognition provided tasks are sufficiently challenging, build on firm pupil subject knowledge, are realistic, and are suitably guided and supported by me.					
I ensure time is given to practise the use of these new skills.					
I provide support (only when it is needed to ensure the transference of skills towards independent use).					

7: Structured Reflection	Rating: 1 - rarely 5 - almost always				
	1	2	3	4	5
I encourage pupils to reflect on the task.					
I encourage students to reflect on how successfully they applied the strategy.					
I encourage students to reflect on how they might use it in the future.					

Figure 7.6 Identifying my strengths and small changes I can make questionnaire

Identifying my strengths and small changes I can make:

How confident are you in knowing what a strategy is and how you can teach one? Where would you position yourself in Figure 7.7? How different is this to how you assessed yourself in Figure 7.1?

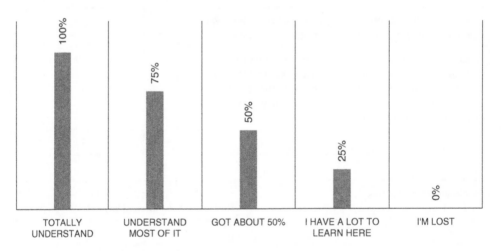

HOW CONFIDENT ARE YOU IN KNOWING WHAT A STRATEGY IS AND HOW YOU CAN TEACH ONE?

Figure 7.7 Self-reflection tool – how confident are you in knowing what a strategy is and how you can teach one?

How could you improve how you introduce a new strategy?

How do you/could you create a collaborative rather than a competitive environment?

How do you/could you convey to pupils the benefit of the lesson?

What other opportunities could you have to use a thinking aloud to model in your classroom?

How could you get children involved in creating anchor charts and posters about the strategies they are learning?

Is there any other way you can reinforce the use of strategies in your classroom? For example, hand gestures?

Once you have thought about these questions, identify one or two areas that you want to enhance. How are you going to do this? What is the easiest way for you to measure your impact?

What am I going to try?	How can I measure impact?

Figure 7.8 Chapter planning tool

You can always come back to this chapter to build on other areas of practice; however, it is better to keep it simple and easy to manage changes by only committing to one or two at a time.

References

Adams, G., & Carnine, D. (2003). Direct instruction. In H. L. Swanson, K. R. Harris, & S. Graham (Eds.), *Handbook of learning disabilities* (pp. 403–416). Guilford Press.

Ahmadi, M. R., & Gilakjani, A. P. (2012). Reciprocal teaching strategies and their impacts on English reading comprehension. *Theory and Practice in Language Studies, 2*(10), 2053.

Baker, L., Zeliger-Kandasamy, A., & DeWyngaert, L. U. (2014). Neuroimaging evidence of comprehension monitoring. *Psihologijske Teme (Psihologijske Teme), 23*(1), 167–181.

Bereiter, C., & Bird, M. (1985). Use of Thinking aloud in identification and teaching of reading comprehension strategies. *Cognition and Instruction, 2*(2), 131–156.

Block, C. C., & Pressley, M. (2007). Best practices in teaching comprehension. In L. B. Gambrell, L. M. Morrow, & M. Pressley (Eds.), *Best practices in literacy instruction* (3rd ed., pp. 220–242). Guilford Press.

Courtney, A., & Gleeson, M. (2010). *Building bridges of understanding: A whole school approach to children's comprehension development.* www.sess.ie/resources/

Davies, D. Jindal – Snape, D., Collier, C., Digby, R., Hay, P., & Howe, A. (2013). Creative learning environments in Education – A systematic literature review. *Thinking Skills and Creativity, 8*, 80–91.

Duke, N. K., & Pearson, P. D. (2009). Effective practices for developing reading comprehension. *Journal of Education, 189*(1–2), 107–122.

The Education Endowment Foundation (2020). https://educationendowmentfoundation.org.uk/public/files/Publications/Metacognition/EEF_Metacognition_and_self-regulated_learning.pdf

Eme, E., Puustinen, M., & Coutelet, B. (2006). Individual and developmental differences in reading monitoring: When and how do children evaluate their comprehension? *European Journal of Psychology of Education, 21*(1), 91–115.

Haywood, H. C. (1988). Bridging: A special technique of mediation. *The Thinking Teacher, 4*(4), 4–5.

Moir, T. (2017). *Developing higher-order reading skills in mainstream primary schools: A metacognitive approach* [Doctoral dissertation, University of Strathclyde].

Moir, T., Boyle, J., & Woolfson, L. M. (2020). Developing higher-order reading skills in mainstream primary schools: A metacognitive and self-regulatory approach. *British Educational Research Journal, 46*(2), 399–420.

National Literacy Trust. (2021). https://literacytrust.org.uk/

Parrish, S. (2010). *Number talks: Helping children build mental math and computation strategies, grades K-5.* Math Solutions.

Pearson, D., & Gallagher, M. (1983). The instruction of reading comprehension. *Contemporary Educational Psychology, 8*(3), 317–344.

Raphael, T. E., & Au, K. H. (2005). QAR: Enhancing comprehension and test taking across grades and content areas. *Reading Teacher, 59*(3), 206–221.

Shanahan, T., Callison, K., Carriere, C., Duke, N., Pearson, D., Schatschneider, C., & Torgesen, J. (2010). *Improving reading comprehension in kindergarten through 3rd grade. IES practice guide what works clearinghouse.* NCEE 2010-4038. US Department of Education.

Sosu, E., & Ellis, S. (2014). *Closing the attainment Gap in Scottish education.* www.jrf.org.uk/sites/default/files/jrf/migrated/files/education-attainment-scotland-full.pdf

Swanson, H. L., & Hoskyn, M. (1998). Experimental intervention research on students with learning disabilities: A meta-analysis of treatment outcomes. *Review of Educational Research, 68*(3), 277–321.

8 Metacognitive strategies and how to teach them

This chapter has selected some evidence-based metacognitive strategies that can enhance learning. These are the metacognitive strategies that were identified from the studies outlined in Chapters 3 and 4, those identified from James-Burdumy et al. (2009); Shanahan et al. (2010) and then further studied by McCartney et al. (2015), Moir et al. (2020), and Moir (2017). They need to be introduced and taught in the way described in Chapter 7, with the general transfer of responsibility passing from the teacher to the pupil. Each strategy in bold is followed by ideas about how discussion of the strategy could be led. The first strategies mentioned: "visualise", "link to the wider world", and "questioning" have extensive examples illustrating what teaching them could look like in practice. This will hopefully give you ideas around how to implement the other strategies mentioned: "hearing a voice in your head", "rephrasing", "summarising", "hold thoughts in your head", "what to do when you do not understand", "crunch points", and "wondering to yourself" and build practitioner confidence (Ness, 2009).

What is your understanding of these metacognitive strategies? Where would you position yourself in Figure 8.1?

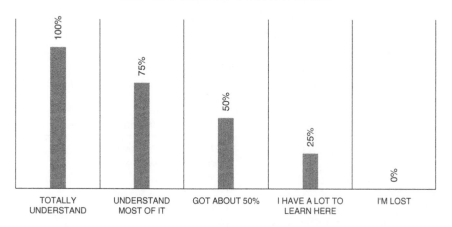

WHAT IS YOUR UNDERSTANDING OF THESE METACOGNTIVE STRATEGIES?

Figure 8.1 Self-reflection tool -- what is your current understanding of the metacognitive strategies "visualise", "link to the wider world", "questioning", "hold thoughts in your head", "what to do when you do not understand", "crunch points", and "wondering to yourself".

DOI: 10.4324/9781003315728-10

For any of these strategies, complete a table in Figure 8.2 to help you implement the strategy. Therefore, here is a blank table to help you do this. The first four strategies have completed tables to model what a completed table may look like. However, if you can think of anything which should be added to the completed tables, please do so.

Strategy	
Ways to nurture this skill	Language to encourage this skill

Figure 8.2 Blank strategy planner

Visualise

This strategy can develop motivation for reading. Choose a book which offers excellent descriptions. After introducing a new book, begin by reading it aloud to the class. Ask the class to imagine the scene and perhaps together draw on the board what this could look like. Add in additional details not mentioned in the book. Get them to describe it in their own words. As you read, continue to populate the picture. Perhaps take out things which you realise are incorrect as you continue reading. Reassure children that their initial picture may have been incorrect, and it is good for a reflective reader to change and update their visualised image as new information is received. Talk about your own experiences which relate to the context, for example, if it is in a wood, what woods have you visited? What was there? What did you hear? What did you smell? Talk about it as though it is a film: "when I read X I want to put X in my movie". Encourage children to link it to their prior knowledge and experience, bearing in mind that all children will have had diverse experiences, so try to be mindful of cultural differences and diversity. Get the children to articulate what they changed or added to their initial visualisation. Reinforce that good readers/problem solvers revise and refine their visualisation "I need to add X to my movie".

Example of completed table of implementation ideas:

Visualising	
Ways to nurture this skill	Language to encourage this skill
• Visualising by closing your eyes, visualise a place: describe what you see, hear, feel. They note keywords and develop their writing from this. • Watch a silent film and imagine the feelings and story of characters in it. Then compare how different soundtracks affect their stories. • Students visualise and create a story before acting it out. How does this affect you? How exactly does your body move? How could this be different?	What was he/she wearing? Where was he/she sitting? Do you think they could smell anything? Would there be any tastes? What do you think their voice would sound like? What do you think they would wear? What were they doing just before this part of the story? If we were looking down on this scene, what else might we see?

• Try to create the context in your mind e.g. outside at night. Students lie on the ground, pretend to look at the sky and relax. They observe detail in the stars, then close their eyes to imagine how the starry sky may change over decades.	How might the scene look after this had happened?
• Students visualise what it is like to be in a different time relevant to the story, e.g. In the 1920s, what would life be like? What would they wear? What is happening around this time (the Wall Street Crash, the end of World War I)?	Has this happened to anyone else? What was it like?
• Create a setting in which students are more likely to engage. Perhaps seasonal by using Lapland at Christmas time.	What do you think the head teacher would do?
• Give students plenty of time to let their imagination gather ideas.	Do you think you would hear any background sounds? If there was music, what kind of music was playing?
• Use open-ended questions to encourage the development of hypotheses rather than a strict notion of right/wrong: ask "what could be?" and answer unanswerable questions.	What else do you imagine might have happened?
• Suggest to the children that they hear something, for example, an animal or a plane. Then ask what are they feeling/seeing/hearing? What would someone in this situation be wearing? Does it make you feel happy? Relaxed? Sad?	Try to picture all this in your mind – what is missing?
• Give the children stimulus – something unusual to talk about. Together, create a story around the item. Create and recreate it.	
• Imagine different states of mind, For example, when would you be frightened/relaxed/or happy?	
• Display pictures or photos around the class/school that are unusual talking points. Create a story around the pictures. Get the children to discuss what is being said or felt by the people in the photographs.	
• Use guided visualisation or mindfulness as a way of relaxing.	
• Use poems or stories which are open to different interpretations and get children to discuss the differences.	

Figure 8.3 Visualisation strategy planner

Link to wider experiences

We use this strategy because relating information to their own life experiences and knowledge deepens their understanding and can help them develop a deeper understanding of how characters feel or the motivations behind their actions. It makes the text more relatable and therefore more memorable, which makes them become more actively involved. Linking can also help the learner identify new questions about the text. Get the pupils to think about how the text relates to what they already know. What they have read so far? What has happened? What was new to them? Have they learned anything about this context? Would they react in the same way? Encourage them to relate the text/data to themselves – "When I was reading this it immediately reminded me of a time when. . . ." "That's interesting because something like that happened to me".

Example of completed table of implementation ideas:

Making links	
Ways to nurture this skill	Language to encourage this skill
• Get the children to tell stories about similar experiences they have had. • Make lists of the similarities and differences. • Get children to interview each other around a common theme. • Compare pictures children draw of a similar scene – what experiences have made them different? What different links have they made with the scene? • Discuss how an abstract picture or painting could connect with and represent their new knowledge: then design and make a sculpture, something they are familiar with. • Visit a different part of the community. For example, elderly persons care home and interview residents. Try to get children to find out the similarities and differences between residents and then between the residents and themselves. • Visit another school or part of the school and draw comparisons with their own. • Notice connections and links and talk about them explicitly. • Encourage children to explain the links that they identify. • Remind pupils of links between skills and areas of knowledge. • Try to find connections between different random objects. Ask children if they could make any connections between the items. The more diverse the objects, the better. • Try games of word association to link different words and ideas. • Use mind maps to brainstorm different concepts or associated ideas. • Use the vocabulary learning template in Chapter 6 to find out more about words and language links.	• Ask yourself, what is this like, that I already know about? • Can you see a link between what we did last week and what we are doing now? • Can you see any connection between the situations? • Can you see any patterns here? • Can you think of a metaphor for this …? • How does the information fit? • How many ideas can we think of here? • How might knowing X help you do Y? • Now that you know… has it changed how you think about …? • What do you know already that could help? • What does it tell you about? • What else do you know?

Figure 8.4 Link to wider experiences strategy planner

Question

Teachers do 80% of the talking. Ultimately, we want to encourage children to have more discussion than teachers. Preschool children are wonderful at asking questions, yet the amount of questions that they ask drops after attending school. Children come to school with the skills to ask good questions and we want to keep and nurture this skill (Davey & McBride, 1986). Questioning is aimed at developing critical thinking skills and learners' ability to carefully examine learning material (Chapman et al., 1995). For example, an online learner thinks about possible alternatives after reading an online concluding statement. Asking questions at the beginning of learning gives students a purpose for learning and encourages them to focus as they listen for specific information to answer the question (Parker & Hurry, 2007). In so doing, they think more actively during the task. Questioning during learning also helps:

- them explain meaning and review content.
- them think more deeply about text and relate it to other things they have learned.
- organise thoughts.
- become more actively engaged with the text.

Encourage the learner to question as they read: what information they in their head, what makes sense, what do they not know, what questions did they have that they have since been able to answer, what has the author not told them? Get children to use the think aloud technique described in Chapter 7. Model your own thought process: "The title suggested X to me so I wonder why…." or "the cover showed the seashore but this is set in Birmingham; I wonder why the sea is relevant?" After reading, encourage them to check which of the questions are answered.

The type of questions that we are aiming for are more than lower-order "after the fact" questions. Encourage pupils to generate questions that are authentic questions for before, during, and after the fact. Try to have the pupils active in the question asking process. Does this seem likely? Does this "ring true"? Do I understand all of this? Students develop, and attempt to answer, questions about the important ideas in the text while reading by using words such as *where* or *why* to cultivate their questions. Put words that are used to formulate questions (e.g., *where, why*) on index cards and distribute them to students. Possibly have students, in small groups, ask questions using these words.

Figure 8.5 shows an example of completed table of implementation ideas:

Questioning	
Ways to nurture this skill	Language to encourage this skill
• When you hear a child ask a good question, notice it and comment on it. Discuss why it is a good question. • Model good, open, and hypothetical questions.	• "That's a great/interesting/ thoughtful/ insightful question". • "Can you think of any questions that would give us the answer to the mystery?"

Figure 8.5 Questioning strategy planner

Questioning	
Ways to nurture this skill	Language to encourage this skill
• Encourage talking about "big" subjects rather than small talk. Ensure that children are safe to make unusual and creative answers. • Create activities by asking questions rather than giving instructions. • Get children to brainstorm what a good question might be based on what they already know. What do they still need to find out? • Write stimulus questions on posters around the room. • Get children to practise asking questions. • Pretend that you are a toddler and continually ask "why" or "how" and see where the topic goes. • Put any good questions up on the wall and refer to them – when are they going to be good questions again? Is it always a good question? • Research and then discuss the types of questions we have; open, closed, speculative, divergent, clarifying, etc. • Is there a list of questions that the class particularly finds useful for different types of tasks? • Once everyone has asked a question about a topic or text, try to decide together what the top three questions are.	• "I don't really know myself yet. I wonder who we could ask to find out together. What should we ask them?" • "If we had a real astronaut here, who could tell us anything we wanted to know, what would we ask?" • "Is this a good enough answer? Am I missing other information?" • "What would be a better question?" • "What do you think a sports person would ask here?" • "What else do you want to know?" • "What else could this answer mean?" • "What questions did we ask last time? Did that question help?" • "What difference does the answer to this question have on my next questions?"

Figure 8.5 (Continued)

Hear a voice reading aloud in your head

This strategy can help when there are lots of characters in the book. It adds depth to the characters and adds to the enjoyment of reading. Varying the intonation in your voice exaggerates the difference between pieces of information. Also, using expression when reading encourages readers to take their time, become immersed in the story, and in so doing use the punctuation cues to enhance understanding.

Rephrase/ Retell

After each section of a book or just if the text gets difficult, stop and practice retelling the story in your own words. Perhaps talk it though in partners; encouraging discussion will deepen understanding and make the information more memorable.

Summarise

Teach learners what a summary is: that it is a brief description of the main topic or theme of the selection that includes only important points. Allow them to practice organising the information in a clear way. Take pupils through the stages of summarising (Brown & Day, 1983), for example:

- Remove unimportant information.
- Remove extra information.
- Replace a term that puts groups of, for example, events into one term.
- Replace a term that puts a list of categories into one category.
- Determine the author's topic sentence or create a topic sentence if none exists.

Then reflect upon the quality of the summary by considering things like; What do I know so far? What don't I know yet? What do I need to know?

Hold your thoughts as you read

Throughout the reading process, encourage learners to think analytically about the story asking questions like: Could that really happen? Why am I being told this now? How does this information link with Chapter 3?

If you don't understand: stop. Re-read

Being able to monitor our understanding as we read is one of the most important skills of a good reader, one that can recognise they do not understand and stop (Claxton, 2002; Wagoner, 1983). When we stop, we can then look back in the text to where things became more confusing. Re-read from where comprehension broke down. Research shows that young children often believe reading is about decoding text and therefore can carry on decoding text even when comprehension is lost. We need to make sure that they understand that the purpose of reading is to gain meaning and quickly get them into the habit of prioritising comprehension. Children will also often believe that if they lose comprehension, it is because of their inability to understand rather than an incoherent text (Wagoner, 1983). Encourage learners to become critical readers who will also identify when the text has errors in it. Encourage them to identify where the difficulty occurs, what it is, perhaps restate the section in their own words. Together, create a classroom activity where a poster or display is created that details all the strategies that we could use when we get stuck.

If you still don't understand

Do not give up. Look back to where the difficulty became apparent. Are there any words/ concepts that you do not know? How could you check something - in a dictionary, thesaurus, or the internet? Have you had a problem like this before? What other information might you need to understand this problem? This is an opportunity to develop grit and perseverance because this is where real learning is happening.

Think about the "crunch" points

Here there can be crunch points within the story, that is, when could the characters have done something different which could have led to a different outcome? What else could have happened at this time? How do you think it would have impacted the outcome? Alternatively, there may be crunch points within the learning process, that is, how could I have understood this passage better? Could I have used a different strategy? Thinking about alternative approaches to learning will increase the learners' metacognitive knowledge and reflecting on the context of the story will deepen their understanding and critical thinking skills.

Wonder to yourself

Encourage children to predict or guess what will happen in a story. Why do they think so? What evidence for or against do they have? Then look back to see whether these guesses or predictions are correct. Had they missed any information? How did the predictions change as they continued to read and gather more information? Predictions will not always be correct and they should be reassured that this is the case. We want our learners to continue to have the confidence to make wild guesses.

Self-reflection tool

What is your understanding of these metacognitive strategies? Where would you position yourself in Figure 8.6? How different is this to how you assessed yourself in Figure 8.1?

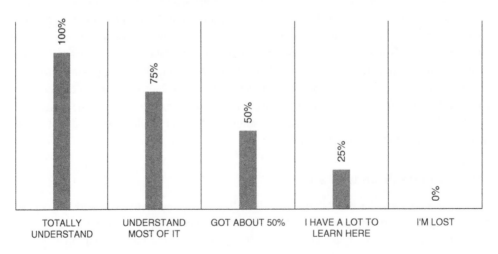

WHAT IS YOUR UNDERSTANDING OF THESE METACOGNTIVE STRATEGIES?

Figure 8.6 Self-reflection tool – how confident are you in these metacognitive strategies having read the chapter?

Which of these strategies have you used before?

Which would best fit your context?

Which metacognitive skills do you think your pupils would benefit from?

Once you have thought about these questions, identify one or two areas that you want to enhance. How are you going to do this? What is the easiest way for you to measure your impact?

What am I going to try?	How can I measure impact?

Figure 8.7 Chapter planning tool

You can always come back to this chapter to build on other areas of practice. However, it is better to keep it simple and easy to manage changes by only committing to one or two at a time.

References

Brown, A., & Day, J. (1983). Macrorules for summarizing texts: The development of expertise. *Journal of Verbal Learning and Verbal Behavior, 22*(1), 1-14.

Chapman, P. F., Crane, M., Wiles, J. A., Noppert, F., & McIndoe, E. C. (Eds.). (1995). Asking the right questions: Ecotoxicology and statistics. In *Report of a workshop held at Royal Holloway University of London*, Egham, Surrey, United Kingdom, SETAC (p. 32).

Claxton, G. (2002). *Building learning power*. TLO Limited Bristol.

Davey, B., & McBride, S. (1986). Generating self-questions after reading: A comprehension assist for elementary students. *The Journal of Educational Research, 80*(1), 43-46.

James-Burdumy, S., Mansfield, W., Dek-e, J., Carey, N., Lugo-Gil, J., Hershey, A., ... Faddis, B. (2009). *Effectiveness of selected supplemental reading comprehension interventions: Impacts on a first cohort of fifth-grade students*. NCEE 2009-4032. National Center for Education Evaluation and Regional Assistance.

McCartney, E., Boyle, J., & Ellis, S. (2015). Developing a universal reading comprehension intervention for mainstream primary schools within areas of social deprivation for children with and without language-learning impairment: A feasibility study. *International Journal of Language & Communication Disorders, 50*(1), 129-135.

Moir, T. (2017). *Developing higher-order reading skills in mainstream primary schools: A metacognitive approach* [Doctoral dissertation, University of Strathclyde].

Moir, T., Boyle, J., & Woolfson, L. M. (2020). Developing higher-order reading skills in mainstream primary schools: A metacognitive and self-regulatory approach. *British Educational Research Journal, 46*(2), 399–420.

Ness, M. (2009). Reading comprehension strategies in secondary content area classrooms: Teacher use of and attitudes towards reading comprehension instruction. *Reading Horizons, 49*(2), 143–166.

Parker, M., & Hurry, J. (2007). Teachers' use of questioning and modelling comprehension skills in primary classrooms. *Educational Review, 59*(3), 299–314.

Shanahan, T., Callison, K., Carriere, C., Duke, N., Pearson, D., Schatschneider, C., & Torgesen, J. (2010). *Improving reading comprehension in kindergarten through 3rd grade. IES practice guide what works clearinghouse.* NCEE 2010-4038. US Department of Education.

Wagoner, S. (1983). Comprehension monitoring: What it is and what we know about it. *Reading Research Quarterly, 18*(3), 328–346.

9 What cognitive strategies should I teach?

There could be a great deal of debate about what constitutes a generic, cognitive, or meta-cognitive strategy (Ahmadi & Gilakjani, 2012; Block & Duffy, 2008). As mentioned in Chapter 3, there is a great deal of overlap and the definition is more aligned to "how" a strategy is used rather than "which" strategy is used. This chapter will look more closely at the other core elements of the intervention outlined in Chapters 3 and 4, that is, those identified from James-Burdumy et al. (2009); Shanahan et al. (2010) and then further studied by McCartney et al. (2015), Moir (2017), and Moir et al. (2020). It will begin by listing some generic skills that can be taught. It is hoped that this will inspire you to think about which skills you might want to consider explicitly teaching. A running theme through this book is the value of explicit teaching of skills; therefore, this chapter will finish by considering how we can support this by outlining both the processes involved in completing a task and giving examples of the end product.

How confident are you in identifying the best strategy for your students? Where would you position yourself in Figure 9.1?

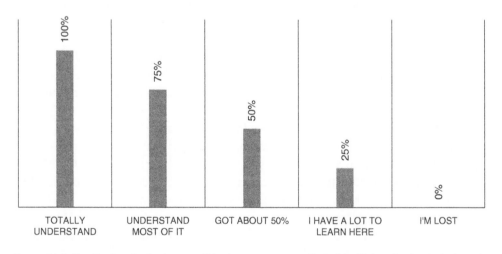

HOW CONFIDENT ARE YOU IN IDENTIFYING THE BEST STRATEGY FOR YOUR STUDENTS?

Figure 9.1 Self-reflection tool – how confident are you currently in identifying the best strategy for your students?

DOI: 10.4324/9781003315728-11

Which strategies should we teach?

There is an abundance of skills that we can teach. The following is a list of some generic skills that could be taught for self-study use. The ones which will be most useful will depend on the task, the subject of qualification that the learner is undertaking. As you look through the list, think which ones would be more relevant to your upcoming lesson or unit. This is not a complete list, so please add to it.

- Synthesising: Here, there is a need to amalgamate or integrate information from a variety of sources. This skill can be subdivided into skills which include: writing an essay/report, reporting findings for a case study, presentation of findings, creating a balanced argument to a problem or design brief, problem solving, designing something, creating a policy or a marketing plan, suggesting improvements on a report/essay/assignment, tackling a typical exam question and creating a plan. How we synthesise will look different for different subjects. For example, in a mathematics class, synthesising may include explaining tasks like trigonometry or linking the similarities and differences of fractions, ratios, and percentages. It may include deciding what kind of calculation or formula is needed to answer the question.
- Evaluation: This can include skills in evaluating an assessment/piece of text/poem/report/a debate/an experiment/case study or plan. There may be a need to estimate outcomes or calculate variations. The skills involved in each of these types of evaluation will have similarities, yet the nuances may need to be tailored. In mathematics, we may evaluate their own or others' mock assessments or comparing and contrasting two solutions, methodologies, or approaches.
- Analysis: Investigating information, breaking down arguments, probing into an enquiry through questioning, considering alternative options/ways of doing things. Perhaps this information can be presented as mind maps, posters, 3D models, and videos. In our mathematics example, this may require establishing the most important points in a problem-solving example or explaining why one method of computation is better than another.
- Study skills: This requires knowing yourself as a learner and taking on board the responsibility to independently employ the strategies and knowledge that you have and transferring this knowledge to situations when you need to (e.g., real-life problem situations or exam conditions).
- Personal skills about myself and how I am feeling as a learner: Being attuned to myself and what motivates me. Here a pupil may be encouraged to think about what they like about the subject, such as mathematics in our example. Alternatively, they could think about why this particular topic might apply to them in the future, for example, counting money/darts scores or how geometry can help us with snooker.
- Social skills: The skills to work with an instructor and to work alongside or with peers appropriately. Specific social skills may also be required if undertaking collaborative

learning, interviewing, or presenting. These skills will also need to translate outside the classroom to help children develop rapport with others.

Structural aids have a mean effect size of d = 0.58. They come in a variety of guises, but all aim to explicitly communicate the structure of what is being learned. Sometimes called "concept mapping" (or mind mapping, spider diagrams, etc.), "advanced organisers" where students are told in advance what they will learn in a lesson or unit, note-taking skills, summary writing or writing frames (Lewis & Wray, 1996; Warwick et al., 2003). This skill of organising data is a key skill in reflective reading (Idol & Croll, 1987).

There are many benefits in using graphic organisers and writing frames, and these include:

- Helping learners identify where to start. For many children, this can be the hardest part of the task when faced with a new task.
- Giving learners an idea of what they are to write. Writing frames are a type of graphic organiser which gives the child an overview of the writing task. These can sometimes have additional information, for example, relevant pronouns (I, you, he, it, etc.) or connecting words to link sentences together.
- Offering relevant connectors or pronouns where necessary can support writers who get stuck writing "and then".
- Children have a better idea of what to do and this raises their motivation to complete the task.
- It gives children an overarching structure for their writing and supports them to see the differences between the different functions of non-fiction writing.
- Reduces copying as children are more able to use the structure to write independently.
- Encourages students to move to higher levels of structuring and expressing their ideas (e.g., bridging a gap between Standard Grade and Higher or Higher plus and degree).
- Frames can have more or less detail so that, if planned appropriately, writing frames are an excellent way of differentiating tasks to meet the needs of all students.

Figure 9.2 is an example of a graphic organiser that a child could use to help them through the process of a mathematical problem. It reminds them of strategies that they can use when they do not know what to do. They start from "read the question", and if they remain stuck, they work clockwise round the diagram, at least, until they are familiar with all the strategies.

However, there are some potential limitations with excessive use of writing frames and organisers:

- They can limit creativity. Writing frames were developed to support non-fiction writing, not creative writing, where learners do not have to stick to the frame.
- The teacher should always be mindful of students becoming too dependent on frames. The frames should provide a basic structure, just enough and no more to

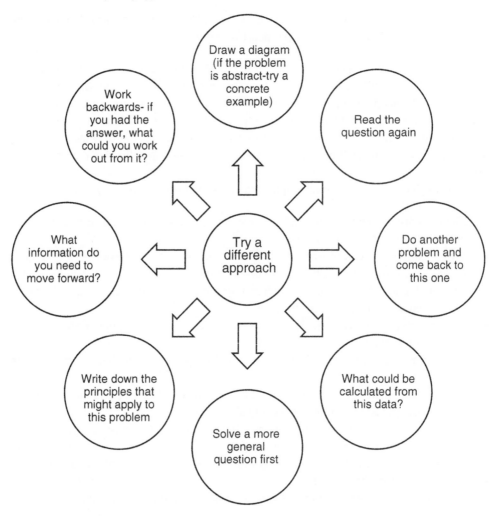

Figure 9.2 A graphic organiser for supporting mathematical problems independently

help the learner on their way. You could get students to create their own writing frames to help them internalise the process and become less reliant on physical frames.

- Becoming too rigid in using frames. Try to allow for adaptation and creativity where possible (Davies et al., 2013).
- There is a danger of over-using writing frames, making learning boring and stagnant.

It is also worth ensuring that any graphic representations that you provide only have relevant information on them, otherwise it can make the process more, rather than less, confusing. Too much on a handout can provide visual overload and therefore handouts need to be tailored to your audience to ensure that they are helpful. Ask your learners for feedback on any new handouts you provide and take on board their feedback. Try to work towards them working through the process independently without the aid. They could work towards creating graphic organisers for other less experienced learners.

Teaching the process and product

It is not enough to teach content (what we need to know). Learners also need to be taught the process, the "how" involved in completing a task (Block & Duffy, 2008; Gail et al., 1994).

Process

The process tells the learner how the task can be done. Here we are outlining the processes that are required for effective use of the skill or completion of the task. When the learner knows about the processes involved, they will know:

- Where do I begin?
- What are the different points or phases within this task?

Therefore, as a teacher, you might want to ask yourself:

- How could I make this process less ambiguous and more overt?
- How can I get students to improve their awareness of this process?

Very often, children find it very difficult to know exactly where to start on a task and once they know this, they will make a good attempt (Baker, 1994). Giving them this information clearly, along with other aspects of the process, will make task completion more accessible and more enjoyable (Sosu & Ellis, 2014).

Learners should also be given guidance to help them know what their end product should look like.

Product

This is where examples of what we want to achieve is made explicit (Rashid-Doubell et al., 2018) the characteristics of the end result. Here you may want to ask yourself:

- How can I exemplify what the end result of the task looks like?
- How can I make clear the features or elements of good work?
- How can learners receive feedback on their attempts?
- Do they have examples of very good or very bad work to check with?
- How can learners get more opportunities to practice the skill?

You could use this flowchart, in Figure 9.3, to help you plan your lesson to ensure that you are explicitly teaching both the process and the product alongside the content.

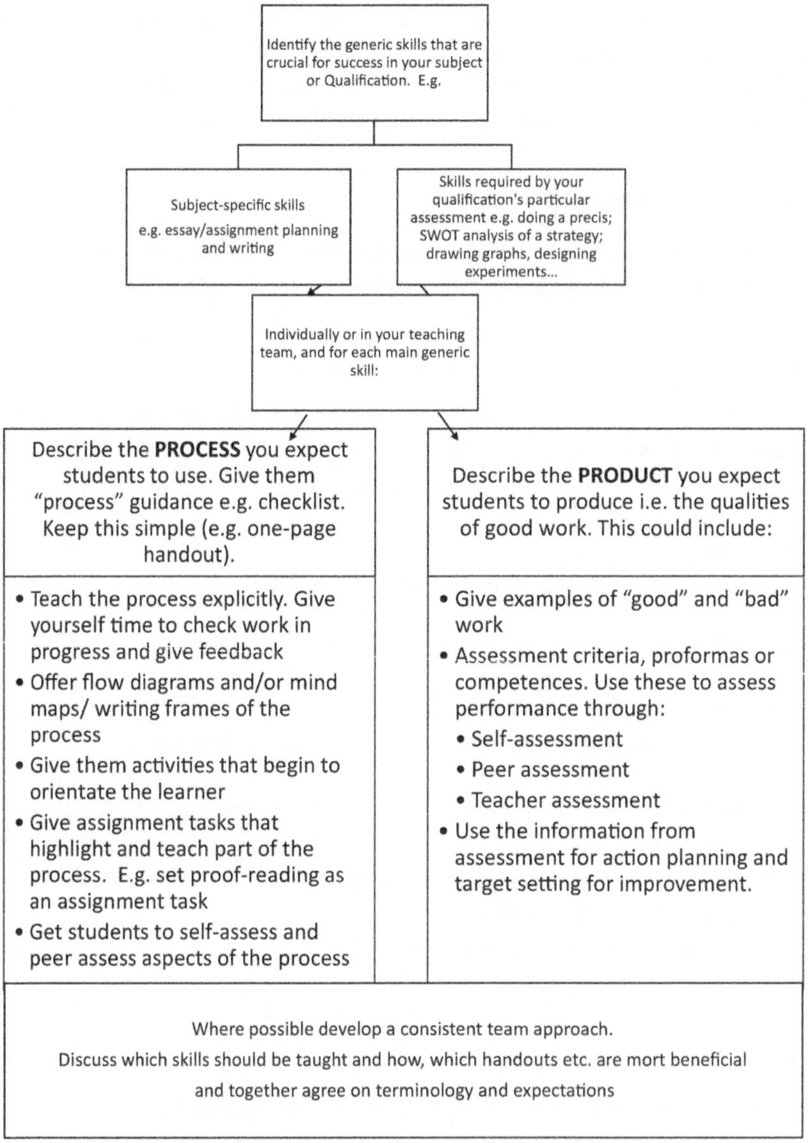

Figure 9.3 Process and product flow chart

The following is one example of process graphic organisers/writing frame. It would need to be adapted to be suitable for your lesson and context. You may need to add detail too.

Process Checklist: Task _____

Date: Name:

Task preparation
☐   Read the title of the task. What does it tell me?
☐   Read the information about the task. Ensure you read all the instructions.

- ☐ Do I understand the task?
- ☐ Re-read the instructions if I do not understand the task.
- ☐ Am I aware of the purpose of the task?
- ☐ How do I feel about the task?
- ☐ Do I have an opinion about the task?
- ☐ Am I focused on the task?
- ☐ What is the task/topic about?
- ☐ What do I know about the task?
- ☐ When is this task due in?
- ☐ Plan when you are going to do the task. Work your plan around other commitments.

Researching

- ☐ Where can I find information that will help with the task? (internet/handouts/ people)
- ☐ Gather information from the different sources.
- ☐ Check the relevance of the information I have gathered.
- ☐ Refer to the task question and check how best to classify my information (e.g., pros/cons, strengths/weaknesses, sub-topics, arguments for and against).
- ☐ Classify the information I have gathered into different subtypes.
  Draw some conclusions about the information I have gathered (e.g., what evidence do I have for or against a position?)
- ☐ Summarise your conclusions.
- ☐ Double check you have sufficient evidence to assert your conclusions.
- ☐ Ask yourself how do you feel as you are progressing? Is your plan to complete this task working? If not, change the plan.

Reporting

- ☐ Re-read the question and ensure that your information will answer every aspect. If not, continue researching.
- ☐ Have all the information you need next to you when working on the task.
- ☐ Plan your report by mind mapping your paragraphs (e.g., Paragraph 1 introduction, paragraph 2 arguments for, paragraph 3 arguments against, paragraph 4 discussion, paragraph 5 conclusions).*
- ☐ Write the report.
- ☐ Re-read the question and ensure that you have answered every section.
- ☐ Leave the report for a couple of days.
- ☐ Reread the question and the report. Ensure that you have answered every section.
- ☐ Proofread for spelling and punctuation.
- ☐ Make necessary changes.
- ☐ Present the report.

Post submission

- ☐ Reflect on the process of doing this: What worked? What did not?
- ☐ What strategies worked well? What did not?
- ☐ What working conditions were useful? Which were not?
- ☐ Where else might I use this learning?

Figure 9.4 An example of a process handout

The tool in Figure 9.4 could also be used to self-assess after completion of a piece of work. Did the student do this activity? If not, why not? It might be useful to discuss whether they stayed with their original plan or did they change it? Also, did they hand the work in on time?

Figure 9.5 is an example of an essay planning proforma aimed at improving a student's process skills. While this one is for writing, you could use planning proforma for many generic skills. However, it is an example only. You may need to adapt this substantially to apply to your context, and to meet the needs of your students. You may need to add detail too.

Write the essay question here: Underline any instruction words (e.g., describe, discuss, assess, do you agree)					
Arguments for	Source of evidence	Order of importance (once all evidence gathered)	Arguments against	Source of evidence	Order of importance (once all evidence gathered)
What is this evidence telling you? Which side of the argument is better supported?					
Organise the evidence above for your report. • Paragraph 1 introduction • Paragraph 2 arguments for • Paragraph 3 arguments against • Paragraph 4 discussion • Paragraph 5 conclusions			Key points for each paragraph: 1. 2. 3. 4. 5.		

Figure 9.5 An example of a product handout

Self-reflection tool

How confident are you in identifying the best strategy for your students? Where would you position yourself in Figure 9.6? How different is this to how you assessed yourself in Figure 9.1?

HOW CONFIDENT ARE YOU IN IDENTIFYING THE BEST STRATEGY FOR YOUR STUDENTS?

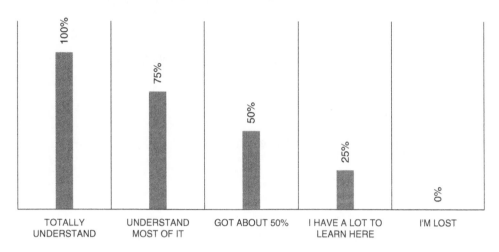

Figure 9.6 Self-reflection tool – how confident are you in identifying the best strategy for your students after having read this chapter?

Which of generic skills apply in your subject?

Can you think of any others?

What do students have repeated difficulty with?

What does the assessment require of them? For example, are there any questions or tasks which are invariably required of them, for example, comprehension, data analysis, and so on?

How could you make this process clearer and more explicit?

How can you get students to improve their use of this process?

How can you make clear the characteristics of good work?

How can you make it clearer what the end result of the task looks like?

How can you give feedback on students' attempts?

Do they have exemplars to check with?

How can you give students more corrected practice in the skill/task?

Once you have thought about these questions, identify one or two areas that you want to enhance. How are you going to do this? What is the easiest way for you to measure your impact?

What am I going to try?	How can I measure impact?

Figure 9.7 Chapter planning tool

You can always come back to this chapter to build on other areas of practice. However, it is better to keep it simple and easy to manage changes by only committing to one or two at a time.

References

Ahmadi, M. R., & Gilakjani, A. P. (2012). Reciprocal teaching strategies and their impacts on English reading comprehension. *Theory and Practice in Language Studies, 2*(10), 2053.

Baker, L. (1994). Fostering metacognitive development. *Advances in Child Development and Behavior, 25*, 201-239.

Block, C., & Duffy, G. (2008). Research on teaching comprehension. In C. C. Block & S. R. Paris (Eds.), *Comprehension instruction: Research-based best practices. Solving problems in the teaching of literacy* (Vol. 2, 2nd ed., pp. 262-281). Guilford Press.

Davies, D., Jindal - Snape, D., Collier, C., Digby, R., Hay, P., & Howe, A. (2013). Creative learning environments in Education - A systematic literature review. *Thinking Skills and Creativity, 8*, 80-91.

Gail, T. E., Lind, G., & -Lebsack, D. (1994). *Teaching writing: Balancing process and product.* Macmillan College Publishing Company, Inc.

Idol, L., & Croll, V. (1987). Story-mapping training as a means of improving reading comprehension. *Learning Disability Quarterly, 10*(3), 214-229.

James-Burdumy, S., Mansfield, W., Dek-e, J., Carey, N., Lugo-Gil, J., Hershey, A., ... Faddis, B. (2009). *Effectiveness of selected supplemental reading comprehension interventions: Impacts on a first cohort of fifth-grade students.* NCEE 2009-4032. National Center for Education Evaluation and Regional Assistance.

Lewis, M., & Wray, D. (1996). *Writing frames.* Reading and Language Information.

McCartney, E., Boyle, J., & Ellis, S. (2015). Developing a universal reading comprehension intervention for mainstream primary schools within areas of social deprivation for children with and without language-learning impairment: A feasibility study. *International Journal of Language & Communication Disorders, 50*(1), 129-135.

Moir, T. (2017). *Developing higher-order reading skills in mainstream primary schools: A metacognitive approach* [Doctoral dissertation, University of Strathclyde].

Moir, T., Boyle, J., & Woolfson, L. M. (2020). Developing higher-order reading skills in mainstream primary schools: A metacognitive and self-regulatory approach. *British Educational Research Journal, 46*(2), 399-420.

Rashid-Doubell, F., O'Farrell, P. A., & Fredericks, S. (2018). The use of exemplars and student discussion to improve performance in constructed-response assessments. *International Journal of Medical Education, 9*, 226-228. https://doi.org/10.5116/ijme.5b77.1bf6

Shanahan, T., Callison, K., Carriere, C., Duke, N., Pearson, D., Schatschneider, C., & Torgesen, J. (2010). *Improving reading comprehension in kindergarten through 3rd grade. IES practice guide what works clearinghouse.* NCEE 2010-4038. US Department of Education.

Sosu, E., & Ellis, S. (2014). *Closing the attainment gap in Scottish education.* www.jrf.org.uk/sites/default/files/jrf/migrated/files/education-attainment-scotland-full.pdf

Warwick, P., Stephenson, P., Webster, J., & Bourne, J. (2003). Developing pupils' written expression of procedural understanding through the use of writing frames in science: Findings from a case study approach. *International Journal of Science Education, 25*(2), 173-192.

10 Successful study skills

This chapter will be concerned with teaching the skills associated with self-studying.

How confident are you in supporting self-study skills? Where would you position yourself in Figure 10.1?

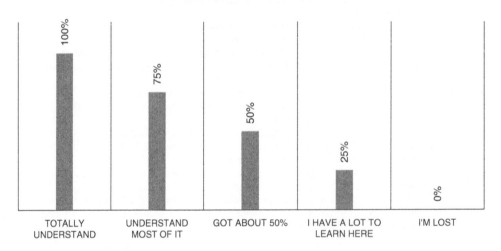

HOW CONFIDENT ARE YOU IN SUPPORTING SELF-STUDY SKILLS?

Figure 10.1 Self-reflection tool – How confident are you in supporting self-study skills?

First, consider how you would define a learner as having good study skills.

The child or young person can be described as successful in study skills when they can self-monitor, self-regulate, and self-assess in a way that ensures they can effectively and independently direct the use of their skills to set targets and achieve their learning goals. They will know what works for them and what does not, and when a strategy does not work, they will change to an alternative approach.

This is a natural process which all independent learners can do quickly and efficiently. It is always best to teach study skills in context. However, this does not mean that the crammed curriculum need worry that time spent on study techniques will eat into their already limited

DOI: 10.4324/9781003315728-12

time. Indeed, while children are practicing their context-specific study skills, they will also learn content. It is rare that a student will spontaneously "transfer" their learning strategies from their use in one subject/context to another (Hattie et al., 1996). An English teacher may have taught a child how to structure an essay, but the child is unlikely to use this approach in history without some additional instruction. It is better to teach study skills using concrete subject examples rather than generalising ideas or keeping the concepts abstract. For example, note taking while reading would be beneficial in the "real life" lesson; or teach essay writing when an essay needs to be written. This integration of subject lesson topic and study skills, with subject-specific activities and materials, will have the greatest impact on both subject knowledge and study skills development.

Before teaching a new subject skill, it may be useful to ask the children to reflect on whether they are aware of the skill. Have they learnt about it before? Is it something they spontaneously do? As with all strategies that the teacher wants to impart, this should be done similarly to that described in Chapter 7 with the gentle transfer of responsibility in a way that begins with clarity around the purpose of the skill, discussion around its application and usefulness, before offering ample opportunity for practice, feedback, and reflection. It is then hoped that this reflective thought will provide the learner with insights to plan how to make their studying even more effective. The more that children take ownership of their own reminders, notes, and structural aids, the more they will understand them and the more meaningful they will be to the learning process. This will better enable them to meet both their short-term study goals and their long-term academic goals (Robbins et al., 2004).

Study strategies

In 2013, Dunlosky analysed the techniques that proved most effective, such as "spaced practice", and the least effective. Taken from the work of Dunlosky, the table in Figure 10.2 summarises the value of the different approaches. More details can be found here: Dunlosky, J. (2013). Strengthening the student toolbox: Study strategies to boost learning. *American Educator*, *37*(3), 12-21.

This is not to suggest that those techniques on the lower part of the table should never be used. Re-reading is essential if comprehension of the text has broken down. Mnemonics can be very useful. You may remember the rainbow colours from the mnemonics Roy G Biv or Richard of York gave battle in vain. Certainly, imagery used for text learning can be a hugely beneficial strategy. When doing my first degree, I had to remember the names and dates of many prominent psychology studies. Inspired by Derran Brown's (2007) memory techniques, I began by listing all the names, dates, with a keyword to remember the studies for each chapter. I then created a "key" for the dates. For example, I would imagine each decade as a distinct pattern (e.g., the seventies were swirls and the eighties polka dots). Each number was a colour (e.g., 3 was red and 4 was blue). This meant, for example, that if a study took place in 1973, my visual would be red swirls. Then I would allocate a familiar room to each chapter, for example, my house or offices. I would then imagine a funny picture in my head that pulled together the colour and pattern that signified the date of the study, plus something that represented the name of the scientist and something about the study.

Effectiveness of ten learning techniques, from Dunlosky (2013)		
High Utility	Practice testing	Self-testing or taking practice tests on material to be learned
	Distributed ("spaced") practice	Implementing a schedule of practice that spreads out activities over time
	Elaborative interrogation	Generating an explanation for why an explicitly stated fact or concept is true
Moderate Utility	Self-explanation	Explaining how new information is related to known information, or explaining steps taken during problem solving
	Interleaved Practice	Implementing a schedule f practice that mixes different kinds of problem, or a schedule of study that mixes different kinds of material, within a single study session.
	Summarisation	Writing summaries of various lengths of to be learned texts
	Highlighting	Making potential important portions of to be learned materials while reading
	Keyword mnemonic	Use keywords and mental imagery to associate verbal materials
Low utility	Imagery use for text learning	Attempting to form mental images of text materials while reading or listening
	Rereading	Restudying text material again after initial reading

Figure 10.2 Effectiveness of ten learning techniques, from Dunlosky (2013)

The more ridiculous the image, the better. I would then imagine these ridiculous pictures around the relevant room for that chapter. It took time to "programme" this, and I made sure I regularly tested my memory, bringing in some of the higher utility approaches to studying material, but it was unbelievable how many facts this system allowed me to remember. Then when the exam arrived, I was completely prepared with all the supporting evidence that I may need for any exam question.

To make any of these study skills real to children and young people, they will need the skill taught, demonstrated, and reminded (Nist & Simpson, 1989). This can be made even more explicit if you use diagrams, thinking out loud, stepping through the strategies, and pretending you are stuck to model what you can do to become unstuck.

When teaching a new skill, give your students practice recognising what they do not understand. The act of being confused and identifying one's lack of understanding is an important part of developing self-awareness (Lavery, 2008). Take time at the end of a challenging class to ask, "What was most confusing about the material we explored today?" This not only jump-starts metacognitive processing, but also creates a classroom culture that acknowledges *confusion* as an integral part of learning.

Other things that can help the learning process:

Higher-order questions

While teaching a new skill, it can also be useful to use questioning techniques. These questions help students to become more aware of their thought processes and how their ideas and opinions have changed and grown. Possible questions might include:

* Before this lesson, I thought clouds were _____. Now I understand them to be _____.
* How has my thinking about pollution changed since working on this topic?

More on questioning and how to question effectively is detailed in Chapter 8.

Learning journals

Personal learning journals help students to monitor their own thinking (Greiner & Karoly, 1976). Part of a class discussion might include identifying weekly questions that help students think about *how* rather than *what* they learned. Questions might include:

* The lesson I felt most comfortable with this week was _____. This was because _____.
* The lesson I felt least comfortable with this week was _____. This was because _____.
* The most challenging thing for me to learn was _____ because _____.
* The study skills I used to greatest effect this week were _____.
* The study skills I used to least effect this week were _____. I will do this differently next time by _____.
* I can become a better learner by _____.
* I can become a better studier by _____.

Encourage creative expression through whatever journal formats work best for learners, including drawings, sketches, mind maps, blogs, wikis, diaries, lists, apps, and so on.

Wrappers

A "wrapper" is an activity which *surrounds* an existing activity. It increases learning and improves metacognitive skills. You might start a lesson by, for example, giving a few tips about effective questioning. After the lesson, get them to write what were the best questions asked during the lesson. Compare their "best questions" with yours. Alternatively, start by giving some tips on how to actively listen. Get the students to write what they thought were the key points from the lesson and then compare their answers with your lesson aims and objectives.

Time management

Another important skill that should be taught explicitly through the seven stages is time management, the ability to plan study time and tasks. For example, an online learner may

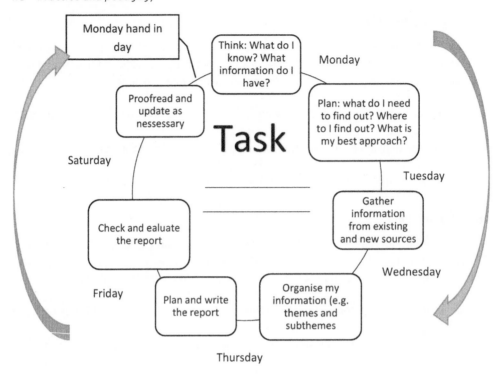

Figure 10.3 Planning clock

schedule a weekly time to read the recommended readings. Figure 10.3 shows a planning clock which children could be coached to use to develop and plan their time management.

Consider assessment types

We really want to encourage our students to think deeply about their learning. Yet, how we assess inadvertently affects the way our students prepare and learn. For example, research shows that students prepare for multiple choice assessments using lower-level thinking, yet higher-level metacognitive skills are used to prepare for essay assessments. While it is less time-consuming to grade multiple-choice questions and students will need experience in answering a variety of types of question, the addition of several short essay questions can expand the way students think about their learning.

Facilitate reflexive thinking

Reflexivity is a metacognitive process whereby we become more aware of our biases (Baker, 1994). Biases can impede healthy development, yet teachers can facilitate a classroom culture of reflexivity by encouraging dialogue that challenges human and societal biases. When students actively become involved in classroom discussion (or assignments) based on moral and ethical dilemmas (e.g., class, politics, sexuality, wealth, race, religion poverty, justice, freedom, etc.), they learn to think about their own thinking and perhaps question and challenge some of their own biases and ideas.

Self-reflection tool

How confident are you in supporting self-study skills? Where would you position yourself in Figure 10.4? How different is this to how you assessed yourself in Figure 10.1?

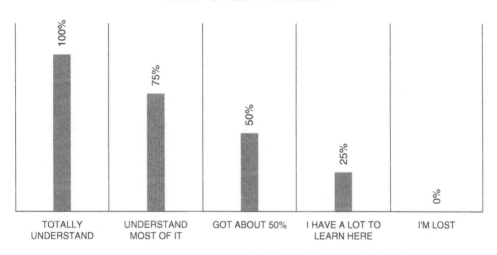

HOW CONFIDENT ARE YOU IN SUPPORTING SELF-STUDY SKILLS?

Figure 10.4 Self-reflection tool – How confident are you in supporting self-study skills after reading the chapter?

What study skills do you find helpful?

Are there any study skills you are going to try?

What other ways do you help students reflect on their thinking in your classroom?

How do you ensure students are taught not just what to do, but how and why?

Which study skills do you think your pupils would benefit from?

Once you have thought about these questions, identify one or two areas that you want to enhance. How are you going to do this? What is the easiest way for you to measure your impact?

What am I going to try?	How can I measure impact?

Figure 10.5 Chapter planning tool

You can always come back to this chapter to build on other areas of practice; however, it is better to keep it simple and easy to manage changes by only committing to one or two at a time.

References

Baker, L. (1994). Fostering metacognitive development. *Advances in Child Development and Behavior, 25,* 201-239.

Brown, D. (2007). *Tricks of the mind.* Random House.

Dunlosky, J. (2013). Strengthening the student toolbox: Study strategies to boost learning. *American Educator, 37*(3), 12-21.

Greiner, J. M., & Karoly, P. (1976). Effects of self-control training on study activity and academic performance: An analysis of self-monitoring, self-reward, and systematic-planning components. *Journal of Counseling Psychology, 23*(6), 495.

Hattie, J., Biggs, J., & Purdie, N. (1996, Summer). Effects of learning skills interventions on student learning: A meta analysis. *Review of Educational Research, 66*(2), 99-136.

Lavery, L. (2008). *Self-regulated learning for academic success: An evaluation of instructional techniques* [Doctoral dissertation, University of Auckland].

Nist, S. L., & Simpson, M. L. (1989). PLAE, a validated study strategy. *Journal of Reading, 33*(3), 182-186.

Robbins, S. B., Lauver, K., Le, H., Davis, D., Langley, R., & Carlstrom, A. (2004). Do psychosocial and study skill factors predict college outcomes? A meta-analysis. *Psychological Bulletin, 130*(2), 261.

PART 3

Implementation at the whole school or authority level

11 Whole school implementation

Some readers may want to implement these ideas within their classroom. Other readers may be school or local government leaders who want to raise attainment more widely. Whoever you are, there are some things within your context which can be facilitators or barriers to effective implementation of these ideas. Hopefully, you will want to share these ideas widely. This chapter is concerned with implementation science, as it can teach us how we can implement any approach effectively.

How confident are you in understanding implementation science? Where would you position yourself in Figure 11.1?

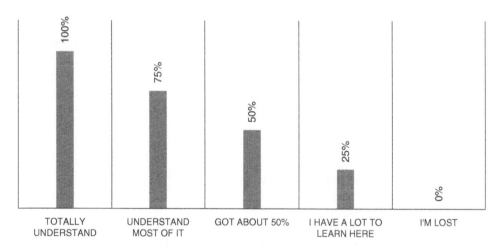

Figure 11.1 Self-reflection tool to identify current knowledge of implementation science

Implementation science

Schools often have limited resources. Therefore, we need to make sure that the money spent on any initiative is well spent. Training staff is costly both in terms of facilitation of venues and

DOI: 10.4324/9781003315728-14

in terms of classroom cover. Add to this the cost of materials associated with a new intervention and the costs increase. Therefore, we need to ensure value for money and we can do this by ensuring that training is cost effective. Thankfully, it is becoming rarer for schools to invest significant sums into interventions that "seem like a good idea". Increasingly, schools recognise the importance of the use of only evidence-based materials and approaches. However, it is unfortunately very common for these interventions, which are grounded in theory and research, to have poorer than expected outcomes (Moir, 2018). Understandably, in such situations, the evidence-based program is discredited by the school and alternative approaches considered. This leads to the big question. How can an evidence-based intervention with solid foundations in empirical research yield poorer than expected results? Implementation science started as the science of these failures (Kelly & Perkins, 2012). Researchers studied what happens when empirically based interventions failed to have successful outcomes in the real world. This chapter considers what implementation science could offer us in ensuring that the evidence-based strategies discussed in this book can be rolled out to have successful results, for implementation science considerations are crucial to the design and evaluation of interventions within education.

Implementation science researchers found that for interventions to have the expected positive impact within the real-world setting, certain core components or variables needed to be observed (Fixsen, Noom et al., 2007). Studies began to recognise that implementation of any new approach necessitated a change in practice and not everyone is open to change because change can be difficult (Fixsen et al., 2009). People need to be open to the prospect of change, and the conditions within which they work are crucial to the sustainability of any newly embedded approach (Moir, 2018). Increasingly, it is acknowledged that success of whole school or authority interventions will only be recognised when implementation science is observed and evaluated throughout the process (Kelly & Perkins, 2012; Spoth et al., 2007).

There are many frameworks, from various specific disciplines, which address implementation (Moir, 2018). The one which we will work through is the Implementation Components Framework (Fixsen, Naoom et al., 2007). This is a conceptual model concerned with fundamental aspects necessary for implementation to be successful (Maher et al., 2009). This identifies the key competency drivers, which are the mechanisms that underpin and therefore sustain implementation:

- Staff selection
- Pre-service/ INSET Training
- Consultation and coaching
- Staff performance evaluation

Organisation drivers are described as the mechanisms to sustain systems environments and facilitate implementation:

- Decision support data systems
- Facilitative administrative support
- Systems interventions

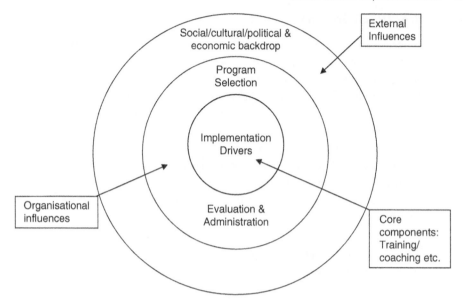

Figure 11.2 Conceptual model of the ecology of implementation

This chapter will continue by looking at each of these drivers as they give a great insight into how the strategies within this book can be rolled out at a whole school level successfully (see Figure 11.2).

Staff selection

If staff morale is low or people are uneasy regarding changes, it is unlikely they will change. The right people to become involved in a new initiative are not necessarily the most experienced. Indeed, Klimes-Dougan's (2009) found in their study of the Early Risers Prevention Programme that staff's personality and not their knowledge or experience predicted the probability of a program being successfully implemented. The best option is staff that are open to change and can stay committed even in the face of challenge – the ones with a growth mindset (see Chapter 5).

When taking the ideas within this book forward, first consider who within your staff has these characteristics to help them drive a new initiative forward. Start by getting a few candidates who are enthused and motivated for positive change and create a dedicated implementation team. This model is widely known with implementation leads, often called "champions". Fixsen, Blase et al. (2007) found designated implementation teams can yield an 80% success in implementation over a three-year period, compared to 14% success over a 17-year period. These champions will ensure that the new intervention does not become diluted or forgotten about.

Pre-service/ INSET Training

In order to ensure a consistency of approach, there will need to be an element of training (Dunst & Trivette, 2009). Changing organisational practices necessitates training. In order to ensure that the training can be best tailored to meet the needs of the trainees, best practice would dictate that a pre-training questionnaire is distributed (Kelly & Perkins, 2012; Moir, 2018). This can measure participants' motivation, readiness, and openness to the training. In addition, it allows the trainer to align the training towards the trainees' needs similarly to how effective formative assessment in the classroom ensures maximum learning by offering an appropriately differentiated session. There is also the possibility of getting information about the school and developing a joint partnership before driving the new agenda forward. Here is an example of a pre-INSET questionnaire with a consent section that was used in the study in Chapter 4.

Developing Reading Comprehension Project
Pre- intervention readiness Questionnaire and Consent

> **This is a measure of staff readiness to engage in training in Developing Reading Comprehension Project to put these principles into practice*.**

	Please tick	
I know about the general aims of The Developing Reading Comprehension Project	YES	NO
I know it is based upon sound research and am confident it is effective in helping children achieve their potential	YES	NO
I know that The Developing Reading Comprehension Project supports their capacity to learn	YES	NO
I am confident I have the time, skills and resources to implement The Developing Reading Comprehension Project effectively	YES	NO
I think The Developing Reading Comprehension Project suits the needs of our primary children	YES	NO
I feel supported by my management in using The Developing Reading Comprehension Project principles and know the time and resources will be available to me to do this well	YES	NO

I know about the general aims of The Developing Reading Comprehension Project	YES	NO
I agree it is important and beneficial to inform parents and involve them in The Developing Reading Comprehension Project	YES	NO
If I need additional coaching in these principles, I know I can request this. Research shows that coaching can boost skills development by 80%	YES	NO
I know that evaluation is crucial, and I will complete the forms provided	YES	NO
I know my comments are highly valued and I will make notes of areas where I think changes could be made or other suggestions about the Developing Reading Comprehension Project	YES	NO
I feel our establishment can commit to carrying out research on the impact of the Developing Reading Comprehension Project curriculum	YES	NO
I do want additional training in the principles of Developing Reading Comprehension Project	YES	NO

Consent

I **DO/DO NOT** (please select) give consent to take part in this research study described in the above information sheet. This will involve implementation of the Developing Reading Comprehension Project, being observed within class and focus groups, prior to, during and following the reading intervention test phase.

Print Name _____

Signature _____

Date _____

Figure 11.3 Pre-intervention readiness questionnaire and consent form

In addition, the quality of overall implementation also depends on how the training is delivered and therefore it is strongly recommended that you have an enthusiastic and committed facilitator.

Consultation and coaching

There is now sufficient evidence that one off training is insufficient when seeking a change in practice. Indeed, one off training is ineffective (Kelly & Perkins, 2012). For genuine change to occur, more than one training session is recommended and in order to translate training into practice, coaching and consultation should take place in between sessions until the new approach has been fully embedded into everyday practice. This model supports continuous ongoing professional development. Peer coaching, with the use of "champions", facilitates the paradigm shift towards new approaches sustainably. Joyce and Showers (2002) found that only 5% of teachers would implement the ideas they had learned in training; however, this soars to 95% if coaching and consultation also took place by a proficient coach. Implementation was maximised when manuals and materials were made available to further support new practices.

Staff performance evaluation

Staff will need opportunities to discuss with colleagues how to embed the new approaches and ideas and therefore it is recommended that discussions for reflection and problem solving take place. If a practitioner has difficulty embedding the ideas, yet does not have the opportunity for discussion, the new approach is likely to be cast aside. Discussion also supports the development of new implementation ideas and, if these sessions are recorded, it will then be possible to further enhance training.

Every new approach or intervention will be founded on a set of ideas. These could be described as the core components, the aspects of the approach that make it what it is (Fixsen, Naoom et al., 2007). Employing an intervention while observing and implementing it as intended is called fidelity (Dane & Schneider, 1998). Every evidence-based intervention will have an effect size. When embedding any new initiative, it is essential that practitioners stay close to the core components, that is, implementing it with fidelity. The impact and positive outcomes will then be at their greatest and nearest to the published effect size. Where considerable adaptations are made, impact and positive outcomes will be at their lowest and farthest from the published effect size (see Figure 11.4). However, research shows that, within education, teachers like to "tinker". This leads to dilution of the intervention and poorer results. One example was given by Greenway in 2002. She studied reciprocal teaching and found it was rarely implemented with fidelity and therefore, it generally had disappointing results. The more the teacher "tinkers", the further it moves away from being evidence based the less likely the positive impact will be realised.

Some interventions are more difficult to implement with fidelity than others. Indeed, Greenway found that implementing reciprocal teaching as intended and as informed by research was challenging. This is therefore another consideration when choosing from evidence-based interventions.

Decision support data systems

During an implementation phase, it will be necessary to monitor the impact and progress using data from a variety of sources including: quality performance indicators, service user

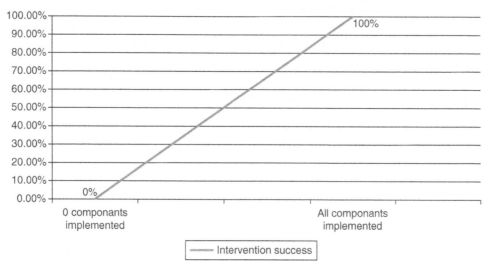

Figure 11.4 The relationship between implementation and intervention success

feedback, and organisational fidelity measures (Fixsen et al., 2005). Fidelity measures include those that check that the programme has the same content, coverage, frequency, and duration as was intended by the researchers/designers. This data can be used to see whether or not the programme is being implemented as intended and if not, something can be done to better ensure the principles are put into practice within the classroom as intended. An example is seen in Chapter 4 Figure 4.2. This graph shows the more an intervention is implemented as intended within the research the more likely the intervention will be successful.

Facilitative administrative support

The leaders of the initiative should keep abreast of how the new initiative sits alongside other agenda's policies and procedures. All policies, agendas, and work plans need to have consistent ethos and values. If the school is trying to implement two inconsistent approaches, staff will get confused and the impact of both will be negligible. An example may be where you have a relationship-based policy running at the same time as a behaviourist "token" system to manage behaviour; or a restorative approach running at the same time as a zero tolerance approach. If your approaches do not align, they cannot be implemented effectively and the messages will be confusing and inauthentic.

Systems interventions

Similar to the internal policies and plans needing a consistency of approach, mindfulness needs to be given to the national policies and agendas. If these external forces for change have differing values to those within the initiative, conflicting messages will become apparent and impact will be negligible. An example is that in Scotland we have the Included, Engaged, and Involved Part 2 Agenda (2017) which aims to reduce exclusions; therefore, a school which takes a zero tolerance approach to behaviour will not sit well within the system and will have less success implementing either the Included, Engaged, and Involved Part 2 Agenda or their zero tolerance school system.

Implementation outcomes for our Chapter 4 example

For our example in Chapter 4, the following implementation outcomes were evident. Findings suggested the results were in line with implementation science. If you refer to this chapter, you will see this is because:

- Staff selection – Where the staff showed an openness to the intervention and the ability to overcome any challenges that may arise during an implementation period (see Chapter 4 Figure 4.6) impact was greatest.
- Pre-service/ INSET Training – Where intervention teachers took part in the training alongside their colleagues and with overt support from the head teacher, intervention teachers had the greatest impact.
- Consultation and coaching – All intervention staff used the modelled examples given within the training to enhance their practice, and this was evident during fidelity observations. Teachers were given access to the researcher throughout the intervention period if they had questions relating to the study; however, they reported that the training session had been sufficient for them to confidently take the intervention forward with the coaching support.
- Staff performance evaluation – Evaluations of performance were given after each fidelity session. These were aimed at supporting the positives of what was working, but also using the core components of the intervention as a tool for discussion to enhance fidelity. Fidelity observation measured criteria increase as the intervention continued, which illustrates the process involved in change. Where there was the greatest fidelity to the intervention, so too, was the greatest impact.
- Decision support data systems – Fidelity was monitored throughout the intervention period. However, it was recognised that to ensure sustainability, support should be ongoing. Similarly to learners needing scaffolding support until the use of strategies become second nature, so to do teachers need coaching support until the new teaching practices become second nature.
- Facilitative administrative support – School policy and systems were all in line with the intervention methodology.
- Systems interventions – local and national polices and systems were all in line with the intervention methodology.

Successful implementation?

Research into what works within schools is crucial as it helps authorities and governments to decide on the best ways to help communities. A programme should be both (1) empirically based and (2) implemented successfully.

There are many evidence-based programmes that can be implemented poorly or they can be implemented well. If implemented poorly, what is seen in the classroom will bear little resemblance to the programme, which yielded evidence-based results, and is therefore going to offer poor outcomes (Moir, 2018). Non-evidence-based approaches could also be implemented poorly or well. In this situation, whether it is implemented well or not, any programme without supporting empirical evidence risks spending valuable time and effort on something that offers no outcomes. Often a glossy initiative has a poor evidence base if you look behind the gloss and many teachers have been fooled into spending a significant amount or money on something that looks nice but has only superficial, inferior quality supporting evidence. The best way of ensuring that you are going to have an impact is by (1) having a programme/intervention/initiative with a sound evidence base AND (2) implementing it in the way that was intended. This can be seen in Figure 11.5, which shows two axes: low to high fidelity and poor in quality evidence base. To ensure optimum positive impact, we are aiming for application of approaches with a robust evidence base being implemented with high fidelity to the programme.

If school leaders recognise its importance, so too will other staff. Therefore, leaders/staff need to be trained on both the new initiative and also the implementation plan. When learning about a new initiative, leaders and those on an implementation team need to know what the crucial elements of the programme are and which aspects can be more suited to fit with the context or environment.

Taking forward any new school priority usually takes more time than is initially negotiated. Research suggests that full implementation can take two to four years (Fixsen et al., 2009), but if implementation is not prioritised and monitored, it could take up to 20 years (Ogden

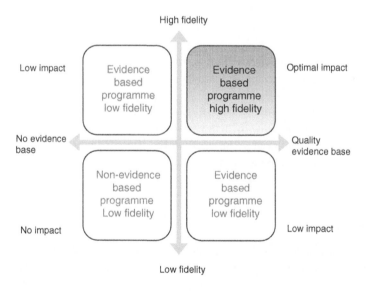

Figure 11.5 It intervention impact

et al., 2012). Yet, often schools have an annual school improvement plan where a priority is only a priority for one school year before moving on to something else. However, if we rush to prioritise too many things, we end up prioritising nothing and our overall general impact is poor. Carroll, Paterson, Wood, Booth, Rick, and Balain's research in 2007 found that the lack of time dedicated to the implementation of new programmes had a significant detrimental impact on the level of fidelity, which adversely affected outcomes. Therefore, before signing up for anything, it is worthwhile having open conversations within the school to decide what it can realistically prioritise well, for it is better to implement one or two things well than to implement several poorly. Implementing only one or two initiatives will also ensure that the components of the initiative are clearer and the staff will feel that adapting to the changes is more manageable.

Implementation with fidelity can feel like an additional hassle, however, ultimately only acknowledging implementation and maximising fidelity when employing an evidenced-based programme will yield the optimum results. Over time, this will be far more cost-effective than poorly implementing lots of different approaches which end up getting abandoned.

To maximise implementation, schools or local authorities should:

- Work in collaboration with schools. Partnership working is best when a relationship is developed between the staff. There should also be opportunities to understand the culture and context within which they work.
- Offer opportunities for discussion about the potential interventions; perform rigorous analysis to ensure programmes are evidence based and meet genuine and not perceived need.
- Measure staff readiness and get the "most ready" candidates to support implementation through steering groups who oversee implementation activities (e.g., fidelity observations/coaching/monitoring).
- Ensure the implementation is designed effectively within the school context.
- Help measure and assess both the impact of the program and its implementation quality.
- Develop implementation standards at a local level (school or local authorities).
- Train staff on the intervention and also its model of implementation.

Change can be difficult, and schools are complex environments, and it can be difficult promoting positive change. Only by being aware of all the needs of staff, internal policies, and external policies/drivers will we be aware of the systems that facilitate progress and or potential barriers. We need to look widely and take this multifaceted approach (Blase et al., 2009).

Self-reflection tool

How confident are you in understanding implementation science? Where would you position yourself in Figure 11.6? How different is this to how you assessed yourself in Figure 11.1?

HOW CONFIDENT ARE YOU IN UNDERSTANDING IMPLEMENTATION SCIENCE?

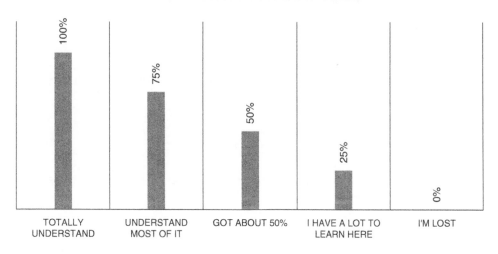

Figure 11.6 Self-reflection tool to identify knowledge of implementation science after reading the chapter

Do you have leadership which supports the implementation of these approaches?

Which staff do you think would be most open to implementing the strategies within this book?

Who could be in your implementation team? Who would lead the team?

Who would be best placed to facilitate training to share the strategies within this book?

Who could be there to coach your staff?

How can you ensure that participants in training have all the materials that they need?

When could you get your staff together to discuss their experience of embedding the strategies and approaches discussed in this book?

What evaluation data could you use to help inform the impact of implementing these ideas and strategies?

What evaluation data could you use to help inform how closely these ideas have been replicated within the classroom?

How can you ensure that your policies and procedures are coherent with the new practices?

Are there any influences from outside the school which are influencing the school's priorities which may impact the implementation of the strategies and ideas within this book?

Once you have thought about these questions, identify one or two areas that you want to enhance. How are you going to do this? What is the easiest way for you to measure your impact?

What am I going to try?	How can I measure impact?

Figure 11.7 Chapter planning tool

You can always come back to this chapter to build on other areas of practice. However, it is better to keep it simple and easy to manage changes by only committing to one or two at a time.

References

Blase, K. A., Fixsen, D. L., Van Dyke, M., & Duda, M. (2009). *Implementation drivers- best practice for coaching*. National Implementation Research Network.

Carroll, C., Paterson, M., Wood, S., Booth, A., Rick, J., & Balain, S. (2007). A conceptual Framework for implementation fidelity. *Implementation Science, 2,* 40.

Dane, A., & Schneider, B. (1998). Program integrity in primary and early secondary prevention: Are implementation effects out of control. *Clinical Psychology Review, 18,* 23–45.

Dunst, C. J., & Trivette, C. M. (2009). Let's be PALS an evidence-based approach to professional development. *Infant and Young Children, 22*(2), 164–176.

Fixsen, D. L., Blase, K. A., Naoom, S. F., & Wallace, F. (2009). Core implementation components. *Research on Social Work Practice, 19,* 531.

Fixsen, D. L., Blase, K. A., Timbers, G., & Wolf, M. (2007). In search of program implementation: 792 replications of the teaching-family model. *Behavior Analyst Today, 8*(1), 96–110.

Fixsen, D. L., Naoom, S., Blase, K., Friedman, R., & Wallace, F. (2005). *Implementation research: A synthesis of the literature*. University of South Florida.

Fixsen, D. L., Naoom, S. F., Blase, K. A., & Wallace, F. (2007, Winter/Spring). Implementation: The missing link between research and practice. *American Professional Society on the Abuse of Children, 19*(1&2).

Greenway, C. (2002). The process, pitfalls and benefits of implementing a reciprocal reading intervention to improve the reading comprehension of a group of year 6 Pupils. *Educational Psychology in Practice, 18*(2), 113–137.

Joyce, B., & Showers, B. (2002). Student achievement through staff development. In B. Joyce & B. Showers (Eds.), *Designing training and peer coaching: Out needs for learning*. National College for School Leadership.

Kelly, B., & Perkins, D. F. (2012). *Handbook of implementation science for psychology in education*. Cambridge University Press.

Klimes-Dougan, B., August, G., Lee, C.-Y. S., Realmuto, G. M., Bloomquist, M. L., Horowitz, J. L., et al. (2009). Practitioner and site characteristics that relate to fidelity of implementation: The early risers prevention program in a going-to-scale intervention trial. *Professional Psychology; Research and Practice, 40*(5), 467–475.

Maher, E. J., Jackson, L. J., Pecora, P. J., Schltz, D. J., Chandra, A., & Barnes-Proby, D. S. (2009). Overcoming challenges to implementing and evaluating evidence -based interventions in child welfare: A matter of necessity. *Children and Youth Services Review, 31,* 555–562.

Moir, T. (2018). Why is implementation science important to intervention design and evaluation, within educational settings? In *Frontiers in education* (Vol. 3, p. 61). Frontiers.

Ogden, F., Bjornebekk, G., Kjobli, J., Christiansen, T., Taraldsen, K., & Tollefsen, N. (2012). Measurement of implementation components ten years after a nationwide introduction of empirically supported programs – A pilot study. *Implementation Science, 7,* 49.

Scottish Executive (2017). *Included, engaged and involved part 2: A positive approach to preventing and managing school exclusions*. The Scottish Government.

Spoth, R., Guyll, M., Lillehoj, C., & Redmond, C. (2007). Prosper study of evidence based intervention implementation quality by community- university partnerships. *National Institute of Health, 35*(8), 981–999.

12 Pupil participation

How confident do you feel in working with children and young people to take forward initiatives? Where would you position yourself in Figure 12.1?

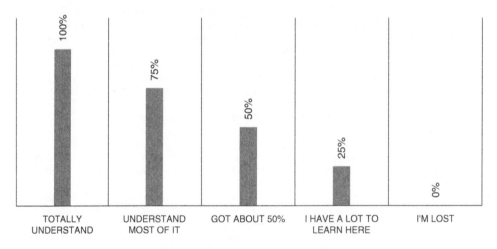

HOW CONFIDENT DO YOU FEEL IN WORKING WITH CHILDREN AND YOUNG PEOPLE TO TAKE FORWARD INITIATIVES?

Figure 12.1 Self-reflection tool - how confident do you feel in working with children and young people to take forward initiatives?

   The approaches within this book often rely on quality discussions and when this was evident, the impact on learning was the same as that of the lesser able as it was for those more able. Therefore, the approach can be defined as universal - it increases the attainment of all. Research shows us that ability groupings have a detrimental impact and interventions which target only certain groups avoid looking at the whole system for whole school improvement.

   Some children will be more eloquent than others. Yet, all children will have opinions about learning and amongst the key principles of the United Nations Convention on the Rights of the Child include the right of children to have freedom to express their thoughts, views, ideas, and opinions in any matter of procedure affecting them (Articles 12, 13-17). By seeking those opinions, listening to children, and discussing their educational preferences, they will feel

DOI: 10.4324/9781003315728-15

valued and included (Brown et al., 2017). As the bond between the learner and the teacher/ school develops, so too does the child's learning potential (Education Scotland, 2018). What if a child has additional needs? How do I take on board what they have to say? There are a myriad of different tools that can ensure that children's and young people's views are taken on board. In doing so, we can build the level of confidence that children have in becoming effective communicators. All children have a voice, and all children should be heard (Brown et al., 2017). This means that our schools need to be inclusive environments if they want to improve learning and teaching (Education Scotland, 2018).

Inclusion

In order for schools to be fully inclusive, the UNESCO advocates four principles:

- "Inclusion is an ongoing process.
- Inclusion is concerned with the identification and removal of barriers.
- Inclusion involves a particular emphasis on those learners who may be at risk of marginalisation, exclusion or at risk of underachievement and,
- Inclusion is about presence, participation, achievement, and support of all learners".

Here we want to encourage our children to participate (Graham et al., 2018). We need to listen to the child's views and ensure that these are incorporated into our planning (Kuurme & Carlsson, 2010; Mannion et al., 2015).

When we talk about inclusive classrooms many tools and approaches are used to ensure that children have a voice. Things like

- Checklists
- Clicker/PECS/Widget/Boardmaker
- Choice or "now and next" boards
- Visual cues, for example, posters/timetables/structural aids
- Audible cues, for example, timers/school bell
- Thinking time
- Widget
- Transitional objects
- Makaton/BSL/singalong/gestures

The intervention discussed in Part 2 of this book highlights the need for teaching to be made explicit – for visuals, checklists, anchor charts, and gestures to be used. Therefore, the approach is very inclusive. As with all learning though, some children will need more explicitness, repetition, and direct teaching than others – yet all children benefit from it and it ensures the most inclusive environment (Kuurme & Carlsson, 2010).

Meeting the needs of children with additional support needs

In ensuring that we effectively meet children's needs, we are not asking questions about the appropriateness of the building. Instead, we are concerned with the people and their skill. Do classroom assistants see themselves as those who save children from all and any adversity?

This classroom assistant will protect the child from harm by creating a cotton wool environment which, while cosy, will never prepare the child for the real world. They cannot see a child struggle when they do not have the answer and therefore will give the child the answer to save them from discomfort. Here, the child receives a message saying that they do not need to try or to employ effort because the classroom assistant will save the day. However, the consequence of this is boredom and disengagement from an uninspiring curriculum. Increasingly, the disengagement will build until the child is of age to drop out of school altogether.

Alternatively, are our classroom assistants those who inspire and facilitate independence? This classroom teacher believes that the child can achieve great things. The classroom assistant will scaffold the child's learning by the minimum amount possible, just enough to edge the child's learning on and no more. There is support, but not so much that creativity and learning are stifled. This means that the child needs to employ effort. The child will know the classroom assistant has high expectations of them and will do everything they can to meet those expectations. They will develop grit. They will see learning as meaningful and worthwhile and aim to fulfil their potential.

Sometimes the lack of resources affects schools' capacity to be fully inclusive and effectively gain children's voices meaningfully. There can be a repetition of exclusion where a child visibly looks included within the mainstream context, yet their school day is differentiated to such a high degree that it bears little resemblance to that of their peers. To deny that any improvement towards a more inclusive environment can be done could be regarded as a very "fixed mindset" approach. Even when resources are limited, consider "how" we do things in schools rather than "what" we do in schools. What messages do the displays and policies inadvertently give? How can you make better use of the resources that are available? How can we manage what we have more creatively? Instead of focusing on the ability of children, focus on the relationship between them. In order for authentic inclusive practices to exist, there must be mixed ability groupings. Expect differences between children.

In a Scottish review of pupils with additional support needs, children were keen to be seen and treated no differently than their classmates (Scottish Government, 2020). Supporting children in schools does not require labels or diagnosis and, giving a label can often reduce achievement because children can perceive it as an excuse or a reason not to try. Ultimately, children have the right to be part of their community alongside their peers.

The most effective learning aids are those created by the learners themselves, as we all have our own unique way of displaying, organising, and interpreting information (Moir et al., 2020). However, before a learner will be sufficiently skilled to make an anchor chart, take notes, or write a learning plan, they may need a little more scaffolding. This could take the form similar to some examples in Part 2. They may also need some additional tools to start to think about what type of learner they are and what aspects of learning are the most important to them. Children with additional support needs do not often need something different, they just need more direct learning experiences, more overtness, more attuned scaffolding and more reinforcement opportunities to help embed their learning.

Creating goals that motivate

Ask children about their aspirations. Do they have any idea what they want to do after they leave school? If they do, use this information as a hook. For example, if they want to work as a social media influencer yet they are not motivated to read, offer examples of how the skill of reading would be necessary to engage in social media. Tie their hobbies and ambitions to their learning goals and targets. For a child who wants to play with her younger sister but does not like reading, their goal might be to read the younger sister a story. Make the link between learning goals and real life.

Understanding myself as a learner

Give learners the time to identify what study skills are and when they might be described as having good study skills. Have classroom discussions to tease out everyone's study strengths, which could include: having a clear sense of purpose, directing energy towards the task at hand, monitoring and checking progress, setting individual targets, and continually improving. Ask them to reflect on whether they regularly check their work before handing it in, Always? Sometimes? Never?

Get the learners to be honest with you and tell you if you, as the educator, provide sufficient exemplars for them to know how to successfully complete a task. If they say you do, ask whether they use these materials effectively. How could you make them more effective or clearer? How could they use them more effectively?

Have classroom discussions asking questions like: If you face a new task, what would help you know what to do? What works well when you are trying something new?

Teach them some basics about learning

Reassure them that real learning takes time and will take practice. Ensure that they know that it is good to take notes and to look back on those notes. Get children to think about a skill; football, art, dance, or anything that they enjoy and ask them how they got better at it. How much did they practise? Who or what supported this learning? What previous knowledge did they have? Help them get ideas from other learners about what helped them learn better, too.

Talk about learning as a process. Talk about something that you have learnt over time. What were your struggles/achievements and the drivers or influences you had to keep going?

Create a culture where it is recognised that the process of learning is more important than the final answer. If there are mistakes along the way, celebrate it, for this is where the real learning occurs. Have discussions in your class about when you have learnt from your mistakes. Start discussions where learners talk about their mistakes and how it helped them improve, try harder, and get better. Remind learners that saying that you do not understand something is a strength rather than a weakness, because it shows that you want to learn. Remember the mantra: No errors = no challenge = no learning.

If you have high expectations of your learners, they will have high expectations of themselves. They will be more likely to take on board challenges rather than focus on easy work, which is boring and uninspiring.

Talk about the brain and how it can change at three different (chemical, structural, or network levels) when you learn as discussed in Chapter 7. Talk about how learning only takes place at the structural and network levels and this requires practice.

Roger Hart created the "participation ladder" in 1997 to show the incremental stages between manipulation towards more meaningful types of participation with children ultimately being empowered to share ideas and lead discussions. More details can be found in Children's Participation: The Theory and Practice of Involving Young Citizens in Community Development and Environmental Care for UNICEF in 1997. Education Scotland and The

University of Stirling also looked into what constitutes meaningful participation in 2018 and found relationships between teachers and learners were key. Additional key factors were learner well-being, classroom ethos, teaching and learning, teamwork, and citizenship. Scotland's commissioner for children and young people found in 2015 that participation requires an agreement that there was equality within the relationship between all children, irrespective of their age. Also, children were not relying on others being the "masters" of all the knowledge. Instead, they felt empowered that they could be the masters in finding truths. Participation should not be tokenistic – it should be empowering.

Participation in quality learning discussions

It is important to have learning discussions (Graham et al., 2018). These can be around different aspects of learning; for example, before, during, or after a task. Figure 12.2 offers some ideas about what these discussions could be about.

Ensuring quality learning discussions		
Overarching theme	Discussion	Suggested questions
Before a task	How do I feel about learning?	What you want to get out of this learning? Why are we doing this topic? How will it help you achieve your personal goals? What skills do you think it will develop? What has previous feedback/mistakes told you about? What you should concentrate on?
	Planning study time	How can you keep your study schedule as regular as possible? How could you manage disruptions to your study routine?
	Being ready to learn	What makes you ready to learn? When are you most focused on this task? How do you feel about the task? Talk about noticing when you are ready to learn. What could you do to get into a better place to learn? How could you reduce stress and focus on the task? What tasks are you more focused on? Why? When do you tend to be at your best for learning? What helps you learn (e.g., reading the question fully or having all the tools/materials at hand)? What tools and materials might be useful to complete X (e.g., flow diagrams and/or mind maps of the process, checklists, planning proformas, self-assessment tools, exemplars?
During	Staying on track	How often do you stop to check your progress? How often do you visualise the end product? What questions would be good to ask yourself? (e.g., how am I doing? Am I still on task? Do I need to revise my plan? When else might I use these ideas/lessons? What information might be missing?)

	Getting stuck	What can you do to help you when you get stuck? (e.g., imagining a voice in your head as you read, re-read the instructions/question, re-read your data, look for where it became complicated, look back through the information/charts/data you have, refer to relevant tools (number line/ mind map/ checklist), split the question up, ask yourself – what do I already know that can help me, use a reference book/dictionary, check the internet, ask a friend, go to another question and come back to the bit that you are stuck with later).
At the end of the task	Checking your work	What can you do to check your work? (look at any examples, self-assess your work against any criteria given, ensure all sections are complete).
	Reflecting on the process	What would be good reflective questions? (e.g., How did you figure this one out? Which of the strategies in the diagram worked, and why? How (else) could you have figured this out? Which strategy could have worked better and why?
	Evaluating your work	How do you know your work is good? How do you notice what you need to work on? How do you check which skills you have developed? Do you ever consider how the skills could be used for other subjects or tasks?

Figure 12.2 Learning discussions

After learning discussions, it can be useful to encourage children to use some sort of framework like this and put sticky notes under each of the sections in Figure 12.3:

I do not yet understand . . . I need help with. . .	**I completely understand. . . . . . I am making few mistakes here and I can work through those**
I am starting to understand. . . . I need coaching but want to try some on my own.	**I understand very well. . . . I can explain this to others without telling them the answers.**

Figure 12.3 Pupils self-assessment tool

Teachers self-reflection tool

How confident do you feel in working with children and young people to take forward initiatives? Where would you position yourself in Figure 12.4? How different is this to how you assessed yourself in Figure 12.1?

HOW CONFIDENT DO YOU FEEL IN WORKING WITH CHILDREN AND YOUNG PEOPLE TO TAKE FORWARD INITIATIVES?

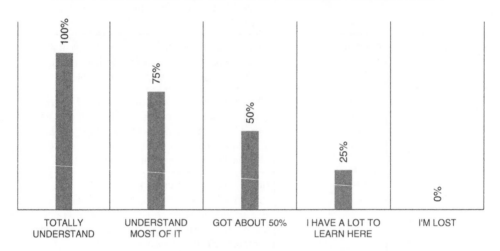

| TOTALLY UNDERSTAND | UNDERSTAND MOST OF IT | GOT ABOUT 50% | I HAVE A LOT TO LEARN HERE | I'M LOST |

Figure 12.4 Self-reflection tool – how confident do you feel in working with children and young people to take forward initiatives after reading this chapter?

How could you best share this information with learners?

How do you gather your pupil's views?

How do you ensure the views of children with complex needs are authentic?

To what extent is your establishment inclusive?

How can the role of staff be defined to ensure that autonomous learning is promoted?

How do you ensure that children are making informed choices?

What has the ethos of additional support been like in your establishment?

Have you got any existing learner groups that could allow for discussion in these areas?

Once you have thought about these questions, identify one or two areas that you want to enhance. How are you going to do this? What is the easiest way for you to measure your impact?

What am I going to try?	How can I measure impact?

Figure 12.5 Chapter planning tool

You can always come back to this chapter to build on other areas of practice. However, it is better to keep it simple and easy to manage changes by only committing to one or two at a time.

References

Brown, J., Croxford, L., & Minty, S. (2017). Pupils as citizens: Participation, responsibility and voice in the transition from primary to secondary school. *CREID Briefing, 34*.

Education Scotland (2018). *Learner participation in educational settings* (pp. 3–18). University of Stirling.

Graham, A., Truscott, J., Simmons, C., Anderson, D., & Thomas, N. (2018). Exploring student participation across different arenas of school life. *British Educational Research Journal, 44*(6), 1029–1046.

Hart, R. (1997). *The theory and practice of involving young citizens in community development and environmental care.* Earthscan.

Kuurme, T., & Carlsson, A. (2010). The factors of well-being in schools as a living environment according to students' evaluation. *Journal of Teacher Education for Sustainability, 12*(2), 70.

Mannion, G., Sowerby, M., & I'Anson, J. (2015). *How young people's participation in school supports achievement and attainment*. Scotlands Commissioner For Children & Young People. SCCYP. http://www.sccyp.org.uk/ufiles/achievement-and-attainment.pdf

Moir, T., Boyle, J., & Woolfson, L. M. (2020). Developing higher-order reading skills in mainstream primary schools: A metacognitive and self-regulatory approach. *British Educational Research Journal, 46*(2), 399–420.

Scottish Government (2020). *Support for learning: All our children and all their potential*. Author.

13 Parental engagement

How confident do you feel in getting support from parents to take forward new initiatives? Where would you position yourself in Figure 13.1?

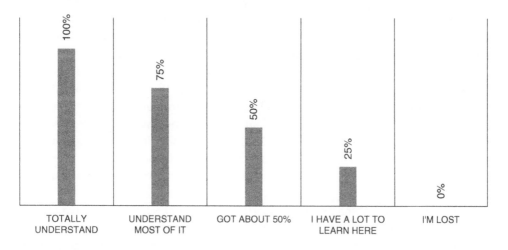

Figure 13.1 Self-assessment around parental engagement

In 2006, in Scotland, the Scottish Schools (Parental Involvement) Act recognised the importance of meaningful engagement and effective involvement with parents and families. This is because if we are all working towards the same goals and using the same approaches to learning, we will develop a joint commitment that increases the likelihood that our children will achieve their potential (North Ayrshire, 2013).

Meaningful engagement

Yet, how do schools meaningfully engage parents? Unfortunately, the readiness for parental engagement varies dramatically between one family and another. Engagement is often

DOI: 10.4324/9781003315728-16

(although not always) better within Early Years settings (Education Endowment Foundation, 2019; Sanabria-Hernandez, 2008) and gradually gets harder and harder as children progress through school. Why is this? Perhaps because parents are more likely to drop off and collect children from the building, therefore making it more likely that positive relationships will develop between Early Years staff and families. Parents will come into the nursery and perhaps help get their child settled in the playroom. This creates opportunities for parental engagement in a natural and integrated way (National Parent Forum of Scotland, 2017). Lessons can be learned from this approach – schools should be forever aiming to create naturalistic ways of integrating parents into the school life throughout the child's school career.

When your school has a change in policy, how is this generally communicated to parents? Is the information clear and specific? Will all parents understand the information? How do you ensure that all parents understand the changes? How do you ensure parents feel comfortable enough to offer truthful feedback? Is this feedback fully taken on board? Many parents lack confidence going into the school territory. They may see staff dressed smartly in suits and get a sense of the hierarchical power systems that can be evident within the school. This can be overwhelming for parents, especially those with negative memories of their own school days. This means parents are unlikely to engage in any meaningful way with the school staff – not because of lack of interest in their child's education but a lack of confidence. The only way to engage such a parent is to build their confidence that the school is not a fearful place and the only way of doing this is by taking a friendly and warm approach, by developing a relationship of openness and trust (Education Endowment Foundation, 2019; North Ayrshire, 2013). We have mentioned in previous chapters the importance of having high expectations for our learners. We also need to have high expectations for our parents, and these positive working relationships can develop where we try (North Ayrshire, 2013). Some parents will need more support than others to effectively engage. The Education Endowment foundation's research (2019) showed that targeted approaches to developing parents' skills and relationships produce higher levels of learning.

Some parents will have had positive experiences at school, while others have not. The value placed in school by the teacher may not be realised by the parent. This makes it difficult to engage with the school because of personal and historical associations which create barriers. The only way to overcome such barriers is by developing positive working relationships, which can be difficult, yet not impossible, for some "harder to reach" parents. Families may come from very different sociological backgrounds to that of the teacher, making it difficult, upon first meeting, to find some common ground. It can take perseverance and effort to prove to the parent that you are working on the same side. Teachers may need support or training to empower them to work with parents who are hard to engage. Yes, some of the most successful work is seen where parents are supported in how to support their children's learning (Goodall & Vorhaus, 2011), especially in the area of literacy (Education Endowment Foundation, 2019), if a parent does not value school, they are unlikely to believe that their child's attendance will support them to make positive life goals. School staff value the school system and recognise its potential to change lives positively. Therefore, we cannot presume that our parents have the same educational goals for their children as we would desire and it is difficult for allies to meet goals that are not shared. We therefore need to talk to our parents to develop an understanding of our different perspectives in order to develop shared goals with our children if any true partnership is to be maintained (Goodall & Vorhaus, 2011). If a parent can feel as though their input is of value or that their feedback is taken seriously, they are more likely to continue to engage.

When involving our parents in consultation, we need to do this meaningfully in a way that encourages a genuine two-way exchange of information (Education Endowment Foundation, 2019).

If we are to get our parents to engage, we need to develop relationships with them. We need to open the lines of communication (National Parent Forum of Scotland, 2017; Scottish Government, 2018). This could include having an introductory session (perhaps with tea and cake) at the beginning of the school year so that parents can get to know you – the teacher. Getting the child to create the invitation can increase parent attendance. The child could write it for any family member of their choosing (not necessarily just Mum and Dad). Mainly it is Mums rather than Dads who get involved, so perhaps ask the parent who rarely attends. Offer them a brief biography of yourself – why you wanted to become a teacher and what your class-wide vision is. You could back this up with a short write up for parents who cannot attend.

Any sort of home/school conversation starter could help. This could take the form of a questionnaire or a home/school link diary. Increasingly, schools and establishments can use online platforms to encourage conversations with parents either through digitally communicated daily learning achievements or through less personalised social media platforms or group chats. These can also have the benefit of enabling families to meet other families, which can make the school seem like an increasingly positive place. Having learning updates where you invite families into the classroom regularly encourages them to truly engage in school matters meaningfully.

Often the only time when a parent is invited into the school is when something has gone wrong. Their child has not behaved as the school would like or their performance in a subject is not as we would like. This can leave the parent (whether or not they are aware of it) with feelings of embarrassment or guilt. If someone continually (although unintentionally) makes us feel bad, it is only natural that we will disengage. Therefore, the only way to keep parents engaging is to communicate with them about far more of the things that are going well and less of the things that are not. If there is a negative that needs to be discussed, we need to be sensitive to the family context. What can be a big issue for the teacher can be an insignificant difficulty within a chaotic family environment. It is best to monitor levels of family engagement and when it appears to dip, try to find out why this might be. Has the communication with home been overly negative recently? Has there been a change of family circumstances? Depending on what these circumstances might be, there may be something that the school can do to improve the situation.

When there is a new approach or school initiative, like that discussed in this book, provide the parent/families with simple guidance about how they can support their child.

Staying in touch

Besides annual school reports, there are a variety of ways to build positive working relationships with parents. These can include:

- Emails, websites, and text services
- Social media
- Encourage membership in the parent council/parent teacher association
- Sessions for input to contribute to policies
- Sessions teaching parents methods and assessment procedures
- Face-to-face informal contact at the beginning or end of day
- Involvement in school reviews and audits
- Letters and newsletters
- Open days/evenings
- School meetings and social events
- Workshops
- Having a parents' room (with a kettle) where parents can meet other parents

Here are some ways you could communicate this approach to developing autonomous learners with parents:

- An information session
- A leaflet
- Inclusion in classroom discussions
- Encourage parents to jointly create an anchor chart with their child
- Encourage parents to jointly create a poster detailing what to do when we get stuck with their child
- Invite your children to teach their parents about a strategy they have learnt and perhaps
- Include parents in discussions with school staff and children to develop learning targets and goals.
- To maximise parental engagement, parents need to feel a connection with the school. Parents love attending the school play but are there other presentations that you could invite your parents to?

What to communicate to parents

The key aspects of the approach within this book that you would want to communicate to parents are:

- Learning takes time. It is a process that requires repetition and reinforcement. Encourage parents to talk to their child about their learning, as this will help them remember it.
- We need to be motivated to learn. When are we/our children most likely to be motivated? How could this be increased? Discuss the different motivation types and why intrinsic motivation is more effective and extrinsic motivations (see Chapter 6)

- Discuss mindset (Chapter 5) and how a growth mindset is instilled when we praise a child's willingness to ask for, and accept, help. Talk about the value of mistakes as they show us what we need to do differently next time to make our work even better.

- Encourage parents to ask their children questions about the process. How did you start this task? What information did you need? How did you work this out? What strategies did you use?

- Encourage parents to ask their children about their learning goals and their study plans. Get them to ask what they would like to achieve, now or in the future. What are their learning goals? How would they like to try and achieve those goals?

- Discuss how children meet expectations and, therefore, the importance of having high expectations for your child.

- Encourage parents to keep learning fun, perhaps by incorporating games and practical activities.

- Encourage parents to support the child's study plan. Get into a routine around when homework takes place.

- Encourage parents to talk to children about how what they are reading or learning connects to their own life.

- Encourage parents not to give answers away when they see their child struggle. Instead, encourage them to discuss with the child what they could do to get "unstuck".

- Encourage parents to ask their child reflective and self-evaluation questions about their learning. Questions like "How am I doing?" "Am I still on task?" "What information do I need?" or "What information might be missing?"

- Encourage parents to remind their children to check their work and wonder how it could be made better.

- Encourage parents to discuss with children the evaluation of a finished piece of work. They could be given prompt questions, for example, "What worked well?" "What do you still need to practise?" "What do you still not quite understand?" "What needs more improvement?"

- If you have provided your learners with exemplars, parents could be encouraged to have discussions with their child about how they compare and contrast with the child's own work.

- Ensure parents understand the importance that it is always best to end on a positive note. Perhaps get them to mention something the child has worked hard at.

- Try to encourage parents to keep calm. We want to create a positive learning environment, not pressure them or our children.

We want to make learning inclusive and keep it fun. We want to ensure our parents are working with us, not against us, and therefore we need to be open and respectful to different families' situations and learning needs. This may mean that some families, like some children, will need more help and support to optimise positive family engagement.

Teacher self-reflection tool

How confident do you feel in getting support from parents to take forward new initiatives? Where would you position yourself in Figure 13.2? How different is this to how you assessed yourself in Figure 13.1?

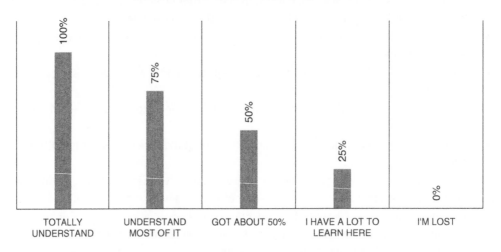

HOW CONFIDENT DO YOU FEEL IN THE AREA OF GETTING SUPPORT FROM PARENTS TO TAKE FORWARD NEW INITIATIVES?

Figure 13.2 Self-reflection tool to identify confidence in parental engagement now having read the chapter

How could you best share this information with parents?

How could you coach them to use these ideas?

Have you got any existing parent/teacher groups that could allow for discussion in these areas?

Once you have thought about these questions, identify one or two areas that you want to enhance. How are you going to do this? What is the easiest way for you to measure your impact?

What am I going to try?	How can I measure impact?

Figure 13.3 Chapter planning tool

You can always come back to this chapter to build on other areas of practice. However, it is better to keep it simple and easy to manage changes by only committing to one or two at a time.

References

Education Endowment Foundation (2019). *Parental engagement'*. https://d2tic4wvo1iusb.cloudfront.net/documents/pages/Parental_Engagement_-_Evidence_from_Research_and_Practice.pdf?v=1631189626

Goodall, J., & Vorhaus, J. (2011). *Review of best practice in parental engagement*. https://dera.ioe.ac.uk/11926/1/DFE-RR156.pdf

National Parent Forum of Scotland (2017). *Review of the impact of the Scottish schools (parental involvement) act 2006*. www.npfs.org.uk/wp-content/uploads/2017/05/Final-E-versionpdf.pdf

North Ayrshire (2013). *Parental involvement strategy (2013)*. www.north-ayrshire.gov.uk/Documents/EducationalServices/parental-involvement-strategy.pdf

Sanabria-Hernandez (2008). *Engaging families in early childhood education*. www.rtinetwork.org/essential/family/engagingfamilies

Scottish Government (2018). *"Learning together" Scotland's national action plan on parental involvement, parental engagement, family learning and learning at home 2018-2021*. https://www.gov.scot/publications/learning-together-scotlands-national-action-plan-parental-involvement-parental-engagement/

14 Professional collaboration and a shout out for educational psychologists

Hopefully going through this book, you have generated a plan of how to take these ideas forwards. Sometimes that can feel overwhelming, in which case I would encourage you to reach out for support from colleagues both within and outside of your school. In addition, think about which other supports you have around you.

What is your understanding of partnership work and peer support? Where would you position yourself in Figure 14.1?

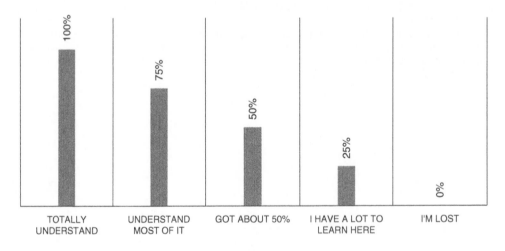

WHAT IS YOUR UNDERSTANDING OF PARTNERSHIP WORK AND PEER SUPPORT?

Figure 14.1 Self-assessment tool – currently how good is your partnership working?

The benefit of partnership working

Schools have many highly skilled teachers, yet research indicates that historically they worked in silos with little meaningful interaction with each other. Yet forging a community of teachers and partners, who together build a culture of community and collaborative

DOI: 10.4324/9781003315728-17

partnership, better supports all towards positive innovation and improvement (Gaskell & Leadbetter, 2009; Hargreaves & O'Connor, 2018). The quality of school collaboration can vary from emerging through to transformational. Ultimately, we want to see progressions towards a transformational professional collaboration where there is an openness to accepting critical feedback which can inform better practice in the future (Hargreaves & O'Connor, 2018). As with all feedback, this should pertain to the lesson or process and not to the characteristics of the person.

To have the biggest impact, partnership groups should have collective autonomy where they explore problems and develop solutions together (Cameron, 2006). They together believe that they can make a difference to learners, have a common meaning and purpose, and quality professional dialogue. The goals of the school need to be clear enough for everyone to see the "big picture".

The partners around a school will vary considerably. It is here that I would like to give a special mention to educational psychologists as they may (obviously depending on your context) be able to support you and your implementation plan (Fixsen & Blase, 2007; Kelly & Perkins, 2012).

Educational psychologists as partners

As with other areas of work, in the past, the Scottish educational psychologist's role was heavily influenced by the Warnock Report (Warnock, 1978; Gilham, 1978) and its emphasis on special educational needs. It used an individual-deficits-based model when considering learning, with minimal strategic work on universal approaches (Baxter & Frederickson, 2005). However, since then, many examples of learning and teaching development work has been led or supported by educational psychologists (EP) within Scotland (Donaldson, 2011; SEED, 2002) and throughout the UK (Ashton & Roberts, 2006; Patrick et al., 2011). This includes the delivery of professional development on evidence-based teaching, collaboration with management about assessment, and supporting the implementation and evaluation of authority-wide learning and teaching programmes (Cameron, 2006; Fixsen & Blase, 2007; Kelly & Perkins, 2012).

Metacognitive skills need to be taught, and teachers may be supported by educational psychologists, who can share their psychological knowledge to enhance implementation with their understanding of evidence-based interventions (Cameron, 2006; Fixsen & Blase, 2007; Kelly & Perkins, 2012).

In schools, many lessons take the same format (Block & Duffy, 2008); this has been criticised for not reflecting the growth that learners make. Indeed, when thinking about learning and teaching, there is a need to acknowledge not just the learning package, but also the:

1. Classroom environment.
2. Quality of teacher explanations in dynamic transactions.
3. Supporting and scaffolding instruction to the individual child.

This learning triad acknowledges the dynamic interplay between teacher, learner, and task, which requires the teacher's individual skill to modify and adapt their approach in an un-prescriptive way, based on the situation. It is no easy feat being a good teacher to all. Teachers' adaptability, flexibility, and creativity need to be capitalised on for pupils to fully benefit from instruction. The goal is to get the balance right: to have supportive teachers who continually monitor individual children's progress and provide supplementary explanations in an "as necessary" way. Rather than imparting knowledge of a strategy, the teacher's scaffolding should teach the child how to become strategic. When a teacher identifies a pupil who is struggling with a metacognitive question, the answer is to scaffold them in using strategies rather than moving on to other pupils who may answer correctly. Therefore, learning how to understand a concept is a far more complex process than the linear one necessary for developing decoding skills. Developing children's comprehension requires a flexible approach, which relies on conversations and the scaffolding of strategy use. This is difficult, and teachers can also benefit from the scaffolding support that discussions with partners provide.

Teachers were not traditionally trained to critique the quality of evidence-based approaches (Cameron, 2006) and therefore may need support from others to do this. There is a danger in schools that decisions around which approach to take are informed by either "what we have always done" or "what is currently in vogue". It takes skilled practitioners to undertake robust research within schools (Eodanable & Lauchlan, 2009). Schools do not offer the scientifically controlled environments that would be ideal for implementing evidence-based approaches (Fixsen & Blase, 2007; Kelly & Perkins, 2012). Working within education requires the understanding of these contexts of unique structures, incorporating powerful dynamics such as relationships, teacher/child/parental beliefs, social pressures, leadership styles, and cultural diversity. Each of these components potentially enhances or limits the reliability of research and the effectiveness of interventions. Educational psychologists and partners can support the complex ongoing process of change, jointly trying to understand these complex interacting variables (Donaldson, 2011; HMIe, 2011), and through the lens of implementation science (Fixsen & Blase, 2007; Kelly & Perkins, 2012).

How Educational psychologists could support schools

Educational psychologists (EP) may support schools through the use of training, consultation, assessment, intervention, and research, and across the levels of the whole school, class, or individual. For example:

1. The EP can support the selection of appropriate evidence-based programmes. EPs can support the ongoing evaluation of impact and outcomes with reference to research (Eodanable & Lauchlan, 2009). They can add a critical lens over qualitative and quantitative information and can compare and contrast intervention approaches to identify that which has the greatest impact (Lindsay, 2008).
2. Teaching is difficult. Teachers often need or want to be supported in the intricacies of how to teach overtly, using a variety of texts, incorporating metacognitive instruction, and making learning more visible through the use of visuals. EPs can provide this

support through training in instruction, which incorporates models of learning, psychological theory, and evidence-based approaches to developing skills (Cameron, 2006).

3. Teachers should have the opportunity to learn how to explicitly teach effective strategies and reflect on their practice. EPs can provide support and opportunities for challenge that support reflective practice and develop teacher efficacy through training and models of coaching and modelling, taking a preventative approach (MacKay, 2002).

4. Within the learning context, the emphasis should not be on assessment of children in order to categorise their skill. Instead, assessment should include an analysis of the teacher, learner, and task within the learning environment. EPs can support teachers in using robust executive assessment frameworks (Kelly et al., 2008; Woolfson et al., 2003) that can support assessment, linking epistemology to methodology to inform practice. EPs can support the implementation of this type of ethos of holistic assessment through systemic consultation, training, and coaching (Boyle & MacKay, 2007; Bronfenbrenner, 1979).

5. For those learners with complex difficulties, the EP, in collaboration, may contribute in a more direct way to holistic assessment of individual need in order to ensure that the correct child's plan is in place (Boyle & Lauchlan, 2009; Bronfenbrenner, 1979).

6. Care needs to be taken to ensure the availability of the right materials such as those that motivate and sustain attention towards fulfilment of personal learning goals. For example, the goal of non-fiction is to extract information, while the goal of fiction is to maintain a creative process for enjoyment and motivation. Therefore, asking children to find reading facts within narrative texts jeopardises their levels of enjoyment and potentially reduces motivation. EPs can support and challenge schools to support the effective selection of materials and resources for specific learning objectives.

7. Learning requires metacognitive behaviour. This means being a strategic learner, one with the ability to control, manipulate, monitor, and regulate cognitive processes in order to pursue our goal of learning. Therefore, EPs could support schools to teach children to think strategically, as this is crucial to successful learning and academic success. Through training, coaching, and consultation, EPs can develop schools' understanding of how to get children to use metacognitive strategies, while also supporting the development of teachers' own metacognitive skills.

Learning can be regarded as a highly complex skill where practice develops automaticity. Opportunities for reflecting on learning and thinking about thinking are therefore essential both as a learner (scaffolded by the teacher) and as teacher (scaffolded by the educational psychologist).

Self-reflection tool

What is your understanding of partnership work and peer support? Where would you position yourself in Figure 14.2? How different is this to how you assessed yourself in Figure 14.1?

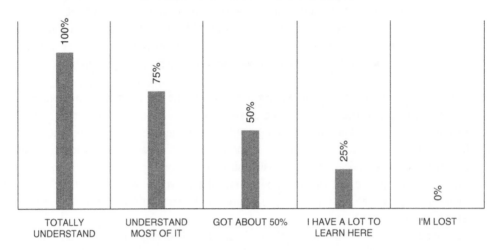

WHAT IS YOUR UNDERSTANDING OF PARTNERSHIP WORK AND PEER SUPPORT?

Figure 14.2 Self-assessment tool – now that you have read the chapter how good is your partnership working?

Who can you go to for help implementing these ideas?

Once you have thought about these questions, identify one or two areas that you want to enhance. How are you going to do this? What is the easiest way for you to measure your impact?

What am I going to try?	How can I measure impact?

Figure 14.3 Chapter planning tool

You can always come back to this chapter to build on other areas of practice. However, it is better to keep it simple and easy to manage changes by only committing to one or two at a time.

References

Ashton, R., & Roberts, E. (2006). What is valuable and unique about the educational psychologist? *Educational Psychology in Practice, 22*(02), 111–123.

Baxter, J., & Frederickson, W. (2005). Every child matters: Can educational psychology contribute to radical reform? *Educational Psychology in Practice, 21*(2), 87–102.

Block, C., & Duffy, G. (2008). Research on teaching comprehension. In C. C. Block & S. R. Parris (Eds.), *Comprehension instruction: Research-based best practices. Solving problems in the teaching of literacy* (Vol. 2, 2nd ed.). Guilford Press.

Boyle, C., & Lauchlan, F. (2009). Applied psychology and the case for individual casework: Some reflections on the role of the educational psychologist. *Educational Psychology in Practice, 25*(1), 71–84.

Boyle, J. M. E., & MacKay, T. (2007). Evidence for the efficacy of systematic models of practice from a cross-sectional survey of schools' satisfaction with their educational psychologists. *Educational Psychology in Practice, 23*(1), 19–31.

Bronfenbrenner, U. (1979). *The ecology of human development: Experiments by nature and design*. Harvard University Press.

Cameron, R. J. (2006). Educational psychology: The distinctive contribution. *Educational Psychology in Practice, 22*(4), 289–304.

Donaldson, G. (2011). *Teaching Scotland's future*. The Scottish Government.

Eodanable, M., & Lauchlan, F. (2009). The advance of research and evaluation skills by EPs: Implications for training and professional development. *Educational Psychology in Practice, 25*(2), 113–124.

Fixsen, D. L., & Blase, K. A. (2007). *Implementation the missing link between research and practice*. NIRN.

Gaskell, S., & Leadbetter, J. (2009). Educational psychologists and multi-agency working: Exploring professional identity. *Educational Psychology in Practice, 25*(2), 97–111.

Gilham, B. (1978). *Reconstructing educational psychology*. Croon Helm.

Hargreaves, A., & O'Connor, M. T. (2018). *Collaborative professionalism: When teaching together means learning for all*. Corwin Press.

HM Inspectorate of Education (HMIe) (Scotland) (2011). *Educational psychology in Scotland: Making a difference: An aspect report on the findings of inspections of local authority educational psychology services 2006-10*. Inspectorate of Education in Livingston.

Kelly, B., & Perkins, D. F. (2012). *Handbook of implementation science for psychology in education*. Cambridge University Press.

Kelly, B., Woolfson, L., & Boyle, J. (2008). *Frameworks for practice in educational psychology: A textbook for trainees and practitioners*. Jessica Kingsley Pub.

Lindsay, G. (2008). *Ethics and value systems. Frameworks for practice in educational psychology* (pp. 52–66). Jessica Kingsley.

MacKay, T. (2002). Discussion paper – the future of educational psychology. *Educational Psychology in Practice, 18*(2), 245–253.

Patrick, H., Anderman, L. H., Bruening, P. S., & Duffin, L. C. (2011). The role of educational psychology in teacher education: Three challenges for educational psychologists. *Educational Psychologist, 46*(2), 71–83.

SEED Scottish Executive, Edinburgh (United Kingdom) (2002). *Review of provision of educational psychology services in Scotland*. Scottish Executive.

Warnock Committee (1978). *Special educational needs: The Warnock report*. DES.

Woolfson, L., Whaling, R., Stewart, A., & Monsen, J. (2003). An integrated framework to guide educational psychologist practice. *Educational Psychology in Practice, 19*(4), 283–302.

15 Some final thoughts

Metacognition: more than just learning

Metacognition plays an important role in all learning, but also within wider life experiences. This means that the impact that a teacher can have in enhancing a child's metacognitive skills can have far-reaching positive outcomes. Beyond academic learning, when pupils gain awareness of their own mental states, they begin to answer important questions:

- How do I live a happy life?
- How do I become a respected human being?
- How do I feel good about myself?

These wider applications of metacognitive skills are beyond the scope of this book. However, it is worth being aware of the impact you can have in supporting the next generation to have the skills necessary to be effective within our world.

Self-awareness plays a critical role in improved learning because it helps students become more efficient at focusing on what they still need to learn. The ability to think about our thinking increases with age. While some research shows that most metacognitive growth happens in adolescence, there is increasing evidence that younger children develop many metacognitive skills. When teachers cultivate students' abilities to reflect on, monitor, and evaluate their learning strategies, young people become more self-reliant, flexible, and productive. Students improve their capacity to weigh choices and evaluate options, particularly when the answers are not obvious. There are some other unexpected gains from teaching self-reflection, for it facilitates better behaviour in 3-4-year-olds. We have looked, in detail, at how we can support the development of these skills which are essential not only for learning but for life.

Look back at the chapters and see what you decided to implement in each of the chapters and plan successful implementation with reference to part 3. Once you have thought about these questions, identify one or two areas that you want to enhance. How are you going to do this? What is the easiest way for you to measure your impact? While teaching strategies well and with sufficient reinforcement takes time, there are simple things you can do right away:

- Display learning progression on walls – not just finished work.
- Model how it feels to be stuck – brainstorm strategies to get unstuck.

DOI: 10.4324/9781003315728-18

- Reward good questions and good answers.
- Explain how learning is a lifelong skill – show how you are still learning.
- Discuss how others overcame difficulties.
- Dual-objectives in class.
- Acknowledge mistakes – and how important they are in learning.

What are you going to do right now?

What am I going to try?	How can I measure impact?

Figure 15.1 Planning first next steps

Index

Note: Page numbers in *italics* indicate a figure on the corresponding page.

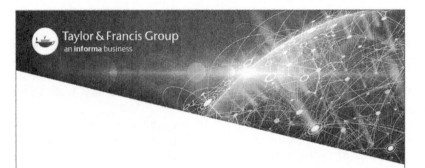